Dedication

Over the years, many people have touched our lives and graced us with support, understanding, advice, encouragement, love, and a safe place to close our eyes. If we had unlimited space (and thought you'd actually read it), we would list every one of them, with the gifts and joys they've given us. Ultimately, we've chosen to honor and acknowledge just two of those people — a teacher who made us better writers and a woman who made us better people.

Rose DiGirolamo Jonez

The funny, brave, generous, fiercely loyal, lovely, kind-hearted, and joyful woman who truly personified the meaning of friendship ... and left us far too soon.

Rose, you are forever loved and deeply missed.

Arnold Levine

The teacher who nurtured our talents, appreciated our humor, shared his joy of life, encouraged our dreams, showed us the beauty and power of words, taught us to think, and, most importantly, never dismissed us as "just girls."

We were lucky to be your students, Arnie;
we're proud you are our friend.
Much thanks from B-40 Jr. High graduating class of '66

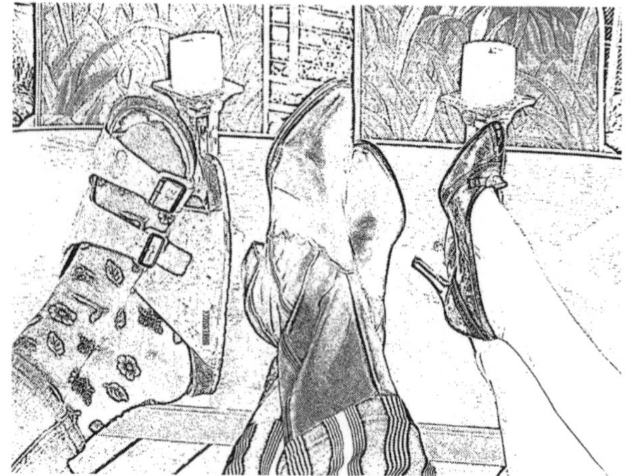

SANTA CRUZ COOKS!

Exploring local restaurants...
one recipe at a time.

The Geezer Chicks' homage to good food, good fun, and good friends

Kathleen Driscoll Hallam   Michele R Reis   Jane Fravel Gordon

GC Publications 2004

ISBN 0-9763317-0-5

Cover illustration and icons by Chris Carothers and Surf City Designs. www.surfcitydesigns.com

Photographs & line art conversion by Michael K. Gordon.

Published by GC Publications, Boulder Creek, California.

Printed in the United States.

Kicking it off...

Welcome to the GC Publications' first born! ***Santa Cruz Cooks!*** is a labor of love (admittedly, often less love and more labor than we had anticipated)—a collection of recipes from our favorite, uniquely Santa Cruz restaurants, coupled with a peek into the world of dining out GC style.

But enough about the book. Wouldn't you really like to know more about us?

GC Publications is the result of friendships formed at Branciforte Elementary School 4+ decades ago when Santa Cruz was a sleepy tourist town of 24,000. We are Geezer Chicks indeed. We were all born and raised right here — and we've been pretty much eating our way around the county ever since. We remember Pacific Avenue's Delmarette and the mountains of pasta at the Santa Cruz Hotel. We remember the Colonial Inn. We remember when home delivery came to Santa Cruz. "Don't cook tonight, call Chicken Delight." And call we did. Not because the luke-cold greasy chicken was all that irresistible, mind you, but rather because we loved seeing that little car under that huge yellow plastic chicken pull into the driveway. We remember at least four restaurants opening (and failing) in a building next to KSCO before someone decided there was perhaps an image problem with a restaurant abutting a slough and tore the whole thing down. We remember root beer floats at the A &W, and carhops punching out (ka-ching, ka-ching, ka-ching) our change from those curious stainless-steel predecessors of the fanny pack. And speaking (writing?) of change, we remember when a budget-busting abalone dinner on the wharf cost $9.99.

Looking back, our best memories of that Santa Cruz childhood all seemed to have some connection to food. And fun. And friends. We realized the memories we're creating now haven't changed all that much. Sure, those few dozen restaurants have grown into a few hundred and our palates have significantly matured, but Santa Cruz is still about food, fun and friends. And what world-class food it is! So that, ladies, gentlemen and gender neutrals, is how the little twinkle in Geezer Chick Kathy's eye gestated into ***Santa Cruz Cooks!***

Santa Cruz County is a culinary melting pot. We have some of the world's best chefs creating the best dishes right here in our own back yard. Sure, we could stay mum and keep them for ourselves, but we believe we have an obligation to share these recipes with the millions of people who eat out of cans and microwaves every day of their lives. Do you realize that today nine out of ten Americans still cook with aluminum pots? And that there are stores still selling coffee in vacuum-sealed tins?

Good food is our heritage, our legacy. Many of our restaurants now sit on the very land that once grew the country's first strawberries, Brussels sprouts, oranges and avocados. When those Neo-colonists were agog over maize, we were already adding artichokes to huevos and creating the earliest-recorded frittata. And that vaunted first Thanksgiving? Santa Cruzans were already dining al fresco year 'round! Our Founding Padres were growing cilantro while your Cajun chefs were still arguing over how to spell coriander and the East Coasters were debating if Cape Cod was named after the fish or vice versa. Now, Geezer Chicks **are** intelligent women. We do realize outsiders might actually think they're eating well, but that's only because they've never been exposed to Santa Cruz area cuisine. Face it, everyone secretly wishes they could eat like us. And now they can.

But what does make Santa Cruz dining so exemplary? Opinions vary. One school credits the climate. Another believes the preponderance of skin-art aesthetic on fellow diners stimulates the taste buds. Still another contends that with all the wine/weed produced and consumed here, everything tastes better. (Curiously, no one has ever suggested these chefs were lured by our low cost of living.) Geezer Chicks have their own theory. Our research has revealed the Santa Cruz restaurant renaissance precisely coincided with the designation of Santa Cruz as a nuclear-free zone. Who knows what subtle toxins and taste twisters were drifting off all those ABMs onto our calamari? Crazy? So when's the last time you saw *Love Canal Canapes Cookbook* or *Three-Mile Island Cooks Organic*? We rest our case.

Whatever the reason, Santa Cruz County is home to a remarkable number of creative chefs, a wide range of dining choices and unique venues. ***Santa Cruz Cooks!*** started with a list of our favorite restaurants. Some were familiar to all three of us; others were closely held "special places" begrudgingly given up for the sake of The Book and the credibility of GC Publications. Some made the list because the food is extraordinary, some made the list because we simply love the physical place, and some offer both exceptional food and a unique dining experience. That original list was eventually pared down, but in truth, we still have our personal favorites and haven't always agreed. We are, after all, Geezer Chicks, not Borg.

Unfortunately, some of our favorite restaurants didn't make it into ***Santa Cruz Cooks!*** A few owners/chefs inexplicably dodged our calls and letters. Others (okay, just one guy off "the farm") asserted this was not the sort of thing he wished to be affiliated with. (We suspect his myopic self read ***Santa Cruz Kooks!***) Several signed on in spirit, but failed to deliver a recipe in time. In the course of working with these restaurants, Geezer Chicks Publications has come to appreciate the pressured frantic schedules of chefs and particularly chefs/owners. Without a track record behind us, we asked these busy people to give of their time and professional secrets. What's truly remarkable is not those who declined, but the generosity of the many chefs and owners/chefs who gave life to ***Santa Cruz Cooks!*** We are deeply indebted to them. We hope our readers living in the area or lucky enough to be passing through will enjoy a meal at one of our participating restaurants. Tell 'em the Geezer Chicks sent ya.

As you read your way through this book, you'll notice improbably shod feathers adding their two cents' worth to the narratives. So what's up with that? Well, for all we have in common, we are three Geezer Chicks with independent opinions, favorites, memories and perspectives. But how best to identify our individual interjections? A conundrum.

We considered getting professional head shots, but decided the cost of air brushing and retouching said photos would be exorbitant.

We considered using our baby pictures. This option guaranteed a Good Housekeeping Seal of Approval and ensured our mothers would buy our books by the gross, but was ultimately nixed when we realized all babies really DO look alike.

Three women, each clever, each a bubble off plumb, but with distinctly different styles. Hmmmm. As we kicked this around, (can you see where we're going here?) we almost simultaneously realized we were kicking with decidedly unique footwear—Kathy, our no-nonsense corporate alpha Chick in exquisitely tooled cowboy boots; Jane, our practical, detail-minded Earth Chick in broken-in Birkenstocks; and Michele, our gregarious, "do I have time for a pedicure?" Chick in strappy stiletto sandals. The seed was planted. The feathers were then a no-brainer. Chicks, writers, quills, yadda, yadda. Prest-o consensus-o, three different feathers wearing three very different pairs of shoes. And speaking their minds. What could be more logical?

It is our hope you will enjoy reading our book, dazzling family and friends with these recipes, and, whenever possible, visiting our participating restaurants. We offer this as the first in a series of Geezer Chicks cookbooks. (Watch for diner, deli, and take-out recipes a la Santa Cruz Cooks 2 Go!) We would appreciate hearing from you and encourage you to send along comments and suggestions.

We encourage you to embrace the essence of Geezer Chick life—good food, good fun, good friends. Enjoy!

The only time to eat diet food is while you're waiting for the steak to cook.

Julia Child

The Restaurants

The Recipes

Breakfast

Appetizers

Soups

Salads & Main Dish Salads

Main Courses

Side Dishes

Miscellaneous

Desserts

Al Boccalino

Tucked in the corner of Aptos Village Square is an Italian jewel, a little ruby decked out with fresh crisp linens, heavy flatware, seasonal produce, and legendary European hospitality. Owners Duncan and Franzika Kerr are meticulous about their service and the quality of their food. Fresh, local, succulent, homemade, expertly spiced describe the Kerrs' offerings.

If you're searching for a repeat of that fabulous pizza you experienced at that quaint little courtyard in Europe, this is the place! I love European pizza—very thin crust, fresh basil, fresh tomatoes, fresh mozzarella, and thinly spread pizzaiola sauce. There is nothing quite as satisfying as this European-style pizza and a glass of red wine to accompany it.

The pizza offerings at Al Boccalino are varied and wonderful. I have set for myself the goal of trying each and every one: Napoletana, Boscaiola, alla Giardiniera... Don't worry about pronouncing them; just focus on devouring them!

If homemade pasta is your dish, there are sixteen different offerings, ranging from homemade gnocchi to the house specialty, Camberi Terra Mare — large prawns with a tomato, wine, and cognac-based cream sauce, served with fresh vegetables and tricolor fussilli pasta.

Dessert is as much a taste treat as the pizza and pasta. Chocoholics will love the Torta di cioccolata, flourless chocolate cake topped with Grand Marnier-flavored whipped cream. Or if you like the traditional, the tiramisu is a must — you will not be disappointed.

They use hormone-free beef here! A definite plus.

Al Boccalino
Aptos Village Square
7960 Soquel Drive, Suite E
Aptos
685-1000

Dinner Mon – Sat
Lunch Mon – Fri
Closed Sun

Al Boccalino's

Penne al Salmone

Ingredients

1 lb penne pasta
400 ml (approximately 16 oz) cream
2 T dry vermouth
zest of half of a lemon
1 can artichoke bottoms
fresh dill
2-3 T grated Parmesan cheese
1/2 t salt
pinch of white or cayenne pepper
200 g (8 oz) smoked salmon (lox)

Preparation

- ✓ Cook pasta al dente, according to manufacturer's directions.
- ✓ Combine cream, vermouth, and lemon zest in a small sauce pan and cook over low heat for approximately 8 minutes.
- ✓ Drain artichoke bottoms and cut into small cubes.
- ✓ Chop the fresh dill.
- ✓ Add the artichoke bottoms, the dill, and the Parmesan cheese to the sauce.
- ✓ Cook for 2 more minutes
- ✓ Add salt and pepper to sauce.
- ✓ Cut salmon into strips.
- ✓ Divide cooked pasta among four plates.
- ✓ Pour sauce over pasta.
- ✓ Garnish with salmon strips.

Serves 4

Aldo's

When Otis Redding sang "Sitting on the dock of the bay.....watching the tide roll away...," he had to have been thinking of Aldo's. With its panoramic view of the yacht harbor, Aldo's is the perfect place for relaxing, sipping a glass of red wine, savoring homemade ravioli stuffed with cheese and fresh spinach, and "watching the ships roll in."

Aldo's is named for Aldo Oliveri, the patriarch of the Oliveri family, one of sixty young families from the tiny Italian village of Riva Trigoso who settled in Santa Cruz after World War I. For over 40 years, "La Barranca" (Santa Cruz's Little Italy) was home to the thriving Italian fishing community. As the small, family-owned fishing business gave way to large business interests, many of the local Italian families switched from catching fish to cooking it. This is why Santa Cruz hosts so many fantastic Italian restaurants. (The Oliveri family owns and operates Sestri as well.)

Aldo's serves great seasonal seafood specialties. Their fish and chips are traditional style, served with tarter sauce and vinegar. And their calamari is claimed to be "The Best in Santa Cruz" — you be the judge on a sunny afternoon with a cold pitcher of beer.

Good food, fresh air, and the joy of being alive is the celebration of the day. As the Italians say, "Giorno per giorno" — take it one day at a time. (Just make sure some of those days are spent at Aldo's.)

This is one of my favorite places to hang out in the afternoon.

An ideal roost for those of use with dinghy envy.

Aldo's Harbor Restaurant
616 Atlantic Ave
Santa Cruz Yacht Harbor
426-3736

Breakfast and lunch daily

Aldo's

Harborside Benedict

Ingredients

1 slice Fugasa bread, split and toasted
1/2 C crab meat
1/4 C Hollandaise sauce
2 soft-poached eggs
cayenne pepper
chopped parsley
parsley sprig
orange slice
salt and pepper mix
side of hash browns or potatoes

Preparation

- ✓ Heat crab meat in a sauté pan with a pinch of the salt and pepper mix.
- ✓ Place Fugasa crust-side down on a plate.
- ✓ Top with hot crab meat.
- ✓ Place poached eggs on crab meat.
- ✓ Place a side of hash browns or potatoes next to the eggs.
- ✓ Top eggs with Hollandaise sauce.
- ✓ Sprinkle Hollandaise with cayenne and chopped parsley.
- ✓ Garnish with parsley sprig and orange slice.

Serves 1

Beach Street Café

I love going to the boardwalk. Always have. I love the energy. The noise. The heart-stopping rides. But there are times when the noise is just too much, when I really don't want fast food for lunch, when I just want to sit and be pampered. Well, right across the street is a little gem that provides the perfect escape. Beach Street Café — an island of tranquility and civilized dining amid a sea of paper-wrapped meals. Serving breakfast and lunch, the Beach Street Café offers an innovative menu that is anything but fast food. (No salt water taffy omelets here!) Owners Willie and Dollie Case use only fresh, wholesome, natural ingredients in their cooking. Their award-winning clam chowder is simmered for hours, and their mile-high hamburger is prepared with care and attention (and probably a few building permits, given that this is Santa Cruz).

Beach Street Café has one of the largest Maxfield Parrish print collections in the United States, and the building dates back to the late 19th century, making it one of the oldest structures in the beach area. So next time, instead of filling up on cotton candy and corn dogs, why not try something different? Head on over to Beach Street Café — for the surprising escape.

The Beach Street Café has wonderful muffins and great coffee.

Beach Street Café
399 Beach Street
Santa Cruz
426-7621

Breakfast and lunch daily

Beach Street Café's

Eggs Sardou

Ingredients

1 lb salted butter
2 t aromat
1 t chopped garlic
1 1/2 C fresh Parmesan cheese, grated
48 oz frozen spinach, thawed
24 to 48 artichoke crowns*
12 eggs
Hollandaise sauce **
paprika
chives, chopped

This recipe serves12 — making it a perfect dish for brunch!

*Canned artichoke crowns are available in most grocery stores.

Preparation

Making the Sardou

- ✓ Melt together first four ingredients. (DO NOT BURN!)
- ✓ Squeeze excess water from spinach and add to pan.
- ✓ Stir and remove from heat.

The Sardou may be made ahead of time and stored for later use.

Assembling the Eggs Sardou

- ✓ Poach the eggs.
- ✓ Place 2-4 artichoke crowns (depending on size) on each plate.
- ✓ Place some of the Sardou mixture on top of the crowns.
- ✓ Top with a poached egg.
- ✓ Ladle an ample amount of Hollandaise sauce over the preparation.
- ✓ Garnish with paprika and chives.
- ✓ Serve with fruit and Mimosas.

Serves 12

** The Beach Street Café Hollandaise sauce is a closely guarded secret. They'll tell you how they make it — but then they'll have to kill you.

Bittersweet Bistro

Located in the old Deer Park Tavern property is the interesting and difficult-to-label Bittersweet Bistro. You'll immediately recognize THIS is not your cookie-cutter bistro. First, there's free parking and lots of it (which is pretty much where any similarity to Deer Park Tavern ends). Off to the left is Bittersweet Express, a smart choice for food on the go or take-out for a leisurely gourmet meal at home.

The magic created by chef/proprietor Thomas Vinolus and his wife, Elizabeth, starts in the charming vine-covered courtyard. Think Cary Grant, Deborah Kerr, Sicily, *Affair to Remember*. Inside you'll find a huge sophisticated dining room. Very crisp, sleek and modern. No attempt to squeeze in extra tables here. Despite its expanse and upscale décor, Bittersweet Bistro retains a feeling of intimacy. Magic. The spotless kitchen opens to the rear of the dining room, but you won't hear any of those kitchen noises. More magic.

There is also a beautiful full bar — rich, dark, walled booths at one end; café tables along a wall of windows at the other; and, in between, a massive, polished mahogany bar. Old Money meets Malibu, and that somehow works, too. Magic.

Two large fresco-walled rooms are available for private events. And the restrooms...I can't comment on His, but, ladies, ours is black marble/chrome, immaculate and well appointed, the starkness mellowed by a small bouquet of red roses. "You could eat off the floor" comes to mind. (Does anyone actually do that?)

The food? Even more magical than the setting. Thomas uses local organic produce and seafood for his creative American Bistro/Mediterranean recipes. And the desserts? Simply exquisite.

Thomas and Elizabeth also host wine tastings, martini Mondays and other events throughout the year. Call or check their website. You won't see hot dogs or grilled cheese sandwiches on the menu, but ask and — voile — magic. Thomas and Elizabeth are happy to accommodate special requests, especially those from kids.

For a memorable dinner, appetizers in the courtyard, or cappucino and a scrumptious dessert at the end of a long day, consider Bittersweet Bistro.

I ate so many appetizers at one of their Wednesday afternoon wine tastings, they had to take me out on a fork lift.

Believe me, It was not a pretty sight.

Bittersweet Bistro
787 Rio Del Mar Blvd.
Rio Del Mar
www.bittersweetbistro.com
831-662-9799

Late lunch and dinner daily

Bittersweet's

Black Beluga Lentil Soup

A great soup on a cold winter night. Or even on a foggy summer night!

Ingredients

2 T olive oil
4 oz bacon, small dice
2 C yellow onion, medium dice
1 C celery, medium dice
1 C carrots, medium dice
1/4 C each yellow, green, and red bell peppers; medium dice
1 Jalapeno pepper, minced (no seeds)
6 oz smoked ham, medium dice
2 T garlic, minced
4 qt chicken stock
2 C tomatoes, chopped (fresh or canned)
3/4 lb black Beluga lentils (brown or French may be used)
1 bay leaf
1 T dried thyme
2 lb yellow Finn potatoes, large dice
2 dashes Tabasco
2 T Italian parsley, chopped
2 T fresh herbs, chopped (such as oregano, sage, rosemary & chives)
1 oz white wine vinegar
salt and paper to taste

Preparation

- ✓ In a two-gallon stockpot over medium heat, add olive oil and bacon, rendering the fat from the bacon.
- ✓ Add onions, celery, carrots, peppers, and jalapeno.
- ✓ Sweat the vegetables until onions turn translucent (approximately seven minutes).
- ✓ Add smoked ham and garlic, and cook for one minute.
- ✓ Add chicken stock, tomatoes, lentils, thyme, and bay leaf.
- ✓ Bring to a boil, and then simmer until lentils are tender.
- ✓ Add potatoes, Tabasco, parsley, fresh herbs, white wine vinegar, and salt & pepper.
- ✓ Simmer until potatoes are tender.

Bittersweet's

Asparagus Salad

with Meyers Lemon Vinaigrette

Ingredients

For the Lemon Vinaigrette

1/2 C lemon juice (preferably squeezed from Meyers lemons)
1 t lemon zest, chopped fine
2 T Dijon mustard
1 C extra virgin olive oil
1/2 C canola oil
1 T honey
One dash Tabasco
Salt & pepper to taste

This recipe serves 8.

For the salad

32 jumbo asparagus spears
2 T olive oil
1 lb mesclun greens
12 oz Parmesan Reggiano

Preparation

- ✓ Preheat oven to 450°.
- ✓ In a nonreactive bowl, combine all of the ingredients for the vinaigrette and whisk until smooth. Season with salt and pepper to taste.
- ✓ Using a vegetable peeler, shave the Parmesan Reggiano into long thin strips.
- ✓ Snap each asparagus spear between your hands, and lightly peel the tip ends.
- ✓ Toss asparagus tips in 2 T of olive oil.
- ✓ Spread the spears onto two rimmed baking sheets.
- ✓ Sprinkle generously with salt & white pepper.
- ✓ Bake ten minutes until spears are cooked al dente.
- ✓ Transfer the spears to a chilled, rimmed baking sheet and refrigerate until cold.
- ✓ Cutting on the bias, slice each asparagus spear into thin, oblong discs.
- ✓ Toss the greens and the asparagus with the vinaigrette.
- ✓ Divide between eight chilled plates.
- ✓ Top with shaved Parmesan cheese and serve immediately.

Bocci's Cellar

In case you're wondering, Bocci's Cellar really is in a cellar. The house on top (which is not part of the restaurant) was originally built at ground level but raised during Prohibition to build the cellar. Why? Because the owners obtained a permit to make "sacramental wine." According to Santa Cruz lore, the local fishermen would gather in the cellar every Sunday, along with their families, where everyone feasted on freshly caught seafood, homemade Italian dishes, and of course, sacramental wine. (Someone had to test it, right?)

Bocci's Cellar no longer serves sacramental wine, but that's about the only limitation of this unique Santa Cruz establishment. The Italian food is still authentic, still delicious, still plentiful. And when you're done eating (or even in between courses), you can always play a quick game of bocci ball in the courtyard. The rules are posted, but that doesn't mean owner Roger and chef Brownie Barnes won't try and hustle you for a game or two.

There's always a ballgame on in the bar, and on Sundays, there's jazz in the courtyard – especially nice on balmy Autumn evenings. And if that isn't enough entertainment, there's Roger himself. Don't be surprised if he comes up to you in his chef whites, looking like a Pillsburini doughboy, and asks, "Does this outfit make me look fat?"

Never a dull moment at Bocci's Cellar. And never a dull meal either. If you haven't given this Santa Cruz landmark a try, you must! (Just don't order the sacramental wine.)

Bocci's Cellar
140 Encinal Street
Santa Cruz
427-1795

Dinner nightly
Lunch Mon – Fri

For its Sunday jazz jams, Bocci's offers $5 pasta plates.
This restaurant is just bursting with personality.

Bocci's Cellar's

Halibut Candiolini

Ingredients

1 halibut filet
pinch salt
pepper
2 cloves garlic, chopped
prosciutto (enough to wrap around filet)
1 C marinara sauce
1 C heavy cream
spinach, raw, tossed with olive oil
olive oil
2 t. lemon juice
white wine (preferably Sauvignon Blanc)

Preparation

- ✓ Preheat oven to 350°.
- ✓ Lay prosciutto on a cutting board and place halibut filet on top.
- ✓ Wrap entire filet in the prosciutto and sprinkle with pepper.
- ✓ In an oven-proof sauté pan, sauté the garlic in a little olive oil.
- ✓ Add halibut filet and brown on both sides.
- ✓ Add lemon juice and white wine.
- ✓ Roast in oven for 12 minutes.
- ✓ Remove from oven and add marinara sauce and cream (about halfway up; do not cover the filet).
- ✓ Simmer 5 minutes.
- ✓ Serve on a bed of spinach.

Serves 1

You can purchase halibut filets from Dave's Gourmet Albacore in Santa Cruz.

Brookroom Restaurant

Hidden away in the redwood forest of the Santa Cruz Mountains, the Brookroom Restaurant at Brookdale Lodge is certainly the most extraordinary dining room in all of California, if not the country. As if the enormous multilevel, gingerbread room, ghosts (yes, you read me right, ghosts; more on this later), and elegantly appointed tables under a massive skylight and exquisite stained glass chandelier weren't breath-taking enough, there's a natural stream coursing through the center of the restaurant! Dubious? Look closely and you'll see trout, crawdads and the occasional salmon. Top that, San Fran-Jewel-of-the-West-Coast-cisco!

The original building at Brookdale Lodge was constructed in1890, and the restaurant added in the 1920s. The Lodge hit its prime in the heady Jazz days. Hollywood heavies like Douglas Fairbanks, Mae West and Tyrone Power be-bopped to head-lining swing bands. Even Herbert Hoover made the trek to this spot, which then had to be about halfway between nowhere and the edge of civilization.

The Lodge fell into disrepair in the 40s, tainted by rumors of Mob connections, secret rooms, tunnels, and even buried bodies. Somehow this tough old dame hung on through abandonment, bad press, floods and a devastating fire, and now new management is restoring Brookdale Lodge to its glory days. So take the drive up Highway 9 and back in time, and treat yourself to an unforgettable dinner or Sunday champagne brunch in the Brookroom Restaurant.

Those ghosts? Well, seems hundreds of people have reported soft jazz, clinking glasses, whispered conversations, and wispy dancing couples throughout the property. But by far the most common sighting is that of Sarah, the young child who drowned in the Brookroom some 60 years ago and now sadly wanders the room at night. Perhaps you faint-hearted types might want to just stick with that sun-drenched champagne brunch...

What did Herbert Hoover say when he saw the Brookroom for the first time?

Brookroom Restaurant
Brookdale Lodge, 11570 Hwy 9
Brookdale, CA 95007
338-6433

Dinner Wed – Sun
Champagne brunch Sun

The Brookroom Restaurant's

Grilled Salmon

with Mango Salsa

Ingredients

8 oz filet of salmon (pin bone out)
3 C mango, peeled and diced
3/4 C red onion, diced
3/4 C roasted red pepper, diced
1 bunch cilantro, chopped
2 C orange juice
1 C chili sauce

Preparation

- ✓ Grill salmon 2 minutes per side.
- ✓ Mix remaining ingredients together.
- ✓ Marinate the salmon in the marinade overnight.
- ✓ Serve over rice with a vegetable of choice.

Serves 1

Café Cruz

I was treating a friend to a birthday dinner, and I asked, "So where do you want to go?" The response was immediate. 'I'd like to go someplace special. How about Café Cruz?" Her assessment—that Café Cruz is special—is indeed shared by many Santa Cruzans. With their delicious food, their fabulous ambience (we had dinner outdoors in March!), and friendly service, Café Cruz has rightfully earned its popularity.

Of course, I'm old enough to remember when this location was the Grape Stake, where diners cooked their own meat. Things are a lot different now—the folks at Café Cruz actually cook the meat for you! And they do it so well. The central rotisserie leaves little doubt that this restaurant takes its grilling very seriously. Which is why my friend's choice was so interesting—you see, she doesn't eat meat. But she had heard about the variety of organic salads at Café Cruz, each a work of art, each featuring the freshest local produce. And we were not disappointed. What a meal!

Café Cruz's New American cuisine is not to be missed. From its smoked meats to its fresh local seafood to its wondrous salads, this is dining Santa-Cruz style.

The bread pudding is absolutely sinful.

Café Cruz
2621 41st Avenue
Soquel
476-3801

Dinner nightly
Lunch Mon – Sat

Personally, I like having the pork chops for dessert.

Café Cruz's

Grilled Skirt Steak

with Summer Vegetable Ragout
and Garlic Mashed Potatoes

Ingredients

2 lbs skirt steak, peeled and cleaned
2 T soy sauce
2 T fresh crushed garlic
1/2 C white wine

Preparation

- ✓ Combine the ingredients for the marinade.
- ✓ Marinate the skirt steak for 4 hours.
- ✓ Grill steak to desired temperature.
- ✓ Slice into 1/2-inch pieces.
- ✓ Place Summer Vegetable Ragout (recipe follows) on bottom of plate.
- ✓ Add a dollop of Garlic Mashed Potatoes (recipe follows).
- ✓ Place skirt steak on top and serve.

Serves 4-6

Café Cruz's

Summer Vegetable Ragout

Ingredients

2 ears fresh white corn, shaved
1 C fresh English peas
1 large summer squash, diced
1 C cherry tomatoes, sliced in half
4 scallions, chopped
1/2 C fresh basil, chopped
1/4 C chicken stock
1 T butter
1 T olive oil
salt and pepper, to taste

Preparation

- ✓ In a large sauce pan, heat the olive oil.
- ✓ Add the corn, peas, squash, tomatoes, and scallions.
- ✓ Sauté for 2-3 minutes.
- ✓ Add chicken stock, butter, and basil.
- ✓ Cook for an additional 2-3 minutes.

Café Cruz's

Garlic Mashed Potatoes

Ingredients

1 lb Yukon gold potatoes
1/4 C butter
1/2 C heavy dream
2 T fresh crushed garlic
2 t kosher salt
1 t white pepper

Preparation

- ✓ Cut the potatoes into chunks.
- ✓ Cook in boiling water until soft.
- ✓ Drain and mash the potatoes .
- ✓ Add remaining ingredients.
- ✓ Whip until smooth.

Café Max

at the Hilton

I recall thinking they were crazy to build a huge hotel in Scotts Valley. It seemed like such a mammoth structure for such a small town. But after sampling the dining at the Hilton's restaurant, Café Max, I'm sure glad they didn't build it elsewhere. (I imagine the planners saying: "*If we build it, they will come ... and eat.*")

Café Max has a wonderfully convenient location for both Santa Cruzans and those of us who live in the mountains. And for me, it's certainly worth a trip down the hill, because Café Max offers superb dining in a cozy, yet upscale, setting.

Chef Mauro Cigarrero offers up a wide variety of California cuisine, including a tasty Chicken Moroccan and one of the best chicken salads around. In fact, all of their salads are terrific. Café Max even provides a senior menu for those who wish more modest portions.

And of course, Café Max offers a full service bar, featuring the best of Santa Cruz wines.

Give it a try. You won't be disappointed!

There are few things cozier than sitting around the fireplace at Café Max.

Well, it'd be a lot cozier if I had a date!

Café Max
6001 La Madrona Drive
(Highway 17 at Mt Hermon Road)
Scotts Valley
440-1000

Dinner nightly
Breakfast & lunch Mon – Fri

Hey, check out the amount of cream in this dessert. No wonder it's so popular.

Café Max's

Crème Brulée

Ingredients

25 eggs
9 C heavy cream
1 1/2 C sugar
1 pinch kosher salt
2 vanilla beans
1 1/2 T vanilla extract

You'll probably want to decrease the size of this recipe. Then again... maybe not.

Preparation

- ✓ Preheat oven to 350°.
- ✓ Separate and beat egg yolks.
- ✓ Heat cream to scalding.
- ✓ Split vanilla beans in half and add to cream.
- ✓ Add sugar, salt, and vanilla extract to cream and mix well.
- ✓ Gradually add the cream mixture to the yolks.
- ✓ Strain into 4-oz (or 6-oz) oven-proof containers.
- ✓ Bake in a baine marie for 30-45 minutes. (Test with a toothpick. The toothpick should come out dry.)

Serves 25

Café Sparrow

You'll find this charming little restaurant right in the center of quaint Aptos Village. (The Geezer Chicks believe any place with wooden plank sidewalks definitely qualifies as "quaint.") The lovely main dining room feels very French Country—bright and sunny, lots of Laura Ashley-esque flowered prints and gingham. On a recent visit, the smaller dining room was the setting for a luncheon of the ladies of the Red Hat Society. Couldn't have been more fitting!

After long stressful years in the restaurant biz (and, for awhile, simultaneously running three restaurants, including Monterey's popular Clawdaddy's on Cannery Row), chef/proprietor Bob Montague and his wife, Julie, now have the restaurant they always dreamed of in Café Sparrow. That dream didn't come without one major hiccup, however. Shortly after opening, the restaurant suffered significant damage in The Quake. Fortunately for us, Café Sparrow proved to be quite a phoenix and has become a favorite of the locals.

The Geezer Chicks suspect you'll feel it the first time you try Café Sparrow and that you'll be back—partly because there are too many tempting choices on the menu and partly because you just feel so darn welcomed and comfortable eating there.

Bob takes full advantage of fresh seafood and local organic produce for his original French bistro dishes, but the true miracle of Café Sparrow is that such wonderful food comes out of such a small kitchen.

Whether for a midweek lunch with the girls, a casual night out with the family, weekend brunch or a romantic dinner for two, you can't go wrong with Café Sparrow—a little place with a big heart.

Café Sparrow
8042 Soquel Dr.
Aptos
831-688-6238

Lunch and dinner daily
Brunch Sunday

My mother-in-law, Helen Hallam, is absolutely hooked on their fresh bread.
Helen is a Geezer Chick Emeritus.

Café Sparrow's

Sesame Seared Ahi Tuna Salad

Ingredients

For the Ahi

4 6-oz portions of very fresh Ahi tuna loin (skin off)
4 T while sesame seeds
4 T black sesame seeds
kosher salt
2 T vegetable oil

For the salad

10 oz fresh baby spinach (thoroughly cleaned)
1/2 C thinly sliced red onion
1/2 C thinly sliced red bell pepper
1/4 C chopped green onion
4 navel oranges, peeled and sectioned
2 T white sesame seeds, toasted
6 oz wasabi vinaigrette

Preparation

- ✓ Preheat a large flat-bottom skillet over medium heat.
- ✓ Mix white and black sesame seeds in a small bowl
- ✓ Liberally salt each tuna loin, and then press into seeds on two sides.
- ✓ Set loins seed side down on a clean dry plate.
- ✓ Oil skillet and heat oil (but do not heat to the smoke point).
- ✓ Place all four loins in the skillet.
- ✓ Sear for approximately 30 seconds.
- ✓ Turn and sear on other seeded side.
- ✓ Remove from skillet to a cutting board and slice thinly with a very sharp knife.
- ✓ In a large bowl, toss all salad ingredients (except sesame seeds) with the wasabi dressing and divide among four entrée salad bowls.
- ✓ Sprinkle toasted sesame seeds on salads and top each with a sliced Ahi tuna steak.
- ✓ Drizzle a little extra dressing on the Ahi.

Did you know?

There are 12 varieties of sparrow. The award for the Most Unnerving Name goes to the Savannah sparrow Passerculus sandwichensis.

I checked with Bob, and he assures me there are no sparrows in his sandwiches.

"Ahi" usually refers to yellowfin tuna.

Wasabi is one of the rarest and most difficult vegetables in the world to grow. Few geographical areas are suited for growing this hot little wonder.

Wasabi is a vegetable that requires careful cultivation. The plant grows to18 inches, producing long stems from the crown of the plant. As the plant ages, the leaves at the base of the stem fall off, and in time a rhizome forms. And this is the part of the plant that becomes wasabi.

Café Sparrow's

Wasabi Vinaigrette

Ingredients

1 t hoisin sauce
1 t honey
2 T soy sauce
3 1/2 oz wasabi paste
1/2 t peanut butter
1/2 T freshly chopped ginger
3/4 C rice wine vinegar
1/4 C vegetable oil
1/2 C sesame oil

Preparation

- ✓ Combine all ingredients and blend well.

Carniglia's

Stefano Carniglia is a third-generation Santa Cruz restaurateur, who believes running a restaurant is simply in his blood. His grandparents migrated to Santa Cruz from the Genovese fishing communities of Riva Trigoso and Sestri Levante. His grandmother, Mary, was the original owner of Miramar (just down the way from Carniglia's), and Steve remembers working on the wharf as a small child.

Carniglia's is Steve's vision of a *locals'* restaurant, an establishment catering to the people who live and work in the county. That's not to say Steve checks your driver's license when you come through the door — tourists are most welcome — but Steve wanted to open a restaurant where locals would gather on a regular basis to enjoy fabulous food, great wine, and panoramic views.

Distinctly Italian salads and pastas, terrific entrees, luscious desserts, and an impressive list of after-dinner drinks. Cognac-infused espresso? Or maybe a grappa is more to your liking.

It's the little touches that make Carniglia's so special. The bread, desserts, and pasta are made on the premises; the herbs are fresh, right out of Steve's garden; and the coffee comes in individual French presses. Now that's class! Not bad for a kid who grew up chasing seagulls along the wharf.

Carniglia's was recently awarded the Wine Spectator's Award of Excellence for their wine list. And what would Italian food be without a spectacular glass of wine?

Carniglia's
Municipal Wharf
Santa Cruz
458-3600

Lunch and dinner daily

By the way, Steve himself may be the best "catch of the day."

Carniglia's

Crespelle al Granchio

(Crab Crepes)

Ingredients

For the crepes
2 eggs
1 C flour
1/2 C milk
1/2 C water
2 oz. olive oil (100%)

For the filling
8 oz Dungeness crabmeat
10 oz ricotta cheese
1 egg yolk
1 oz Parmigiano Reggiano
pinch salt
pinch white pepper
pinch Italian parsley, chopped
2 green onions, diced

Preparation

- ✓ Preheat oven to 450 °.

To make the crepes

- ✓ In a mixing bowl, blend all ingredients (except 1 oz olive oil) until smooth.
- ✓ Using a small, nonstick sauté pan, lightly coat pan with remaining olive oil.
- ✓ Add 2 oz (1/4 C) of mix to pan and sauté until lightly brown (approximately one minute).
- ✓ Flip and finish other side.
- ✓ Set aside until cool.
- ✓ Prepare seven more crepes (2 per person).

To make filling

- ✓ In a mixing bowl, fold all ingredients together.

To assemble

- ✓ Put 2-3 oz of filling into the center of each crepe and then roll.
- ✓ Place crepes in a shallow baking pan (or sauté pan) and bake in oven for approximately 6-8 minutes, until crepe is golden brown.
- ✓ Serve crepes on top of marinara sauce (or your favorite sauce), sprinkled with Parmigiano Reggiano.

Serves 4

Casablanca

It's always a good sign when a restaurant wins multiple awards from The Wine Spectator, a publication that *knows* an impressive wine list when it sees one. I, too, am impressed with Casablanca's wine list. Okay, I'm actually intimidated by it. So many wines and so little time! Still, my point-and-cork method works well enough, probably because it's impossible to go wrong at Casablanca. The extensive wine list is only the beginning. A magnificent view of the Monterey Bay captures my attention every time. And then there's the food.

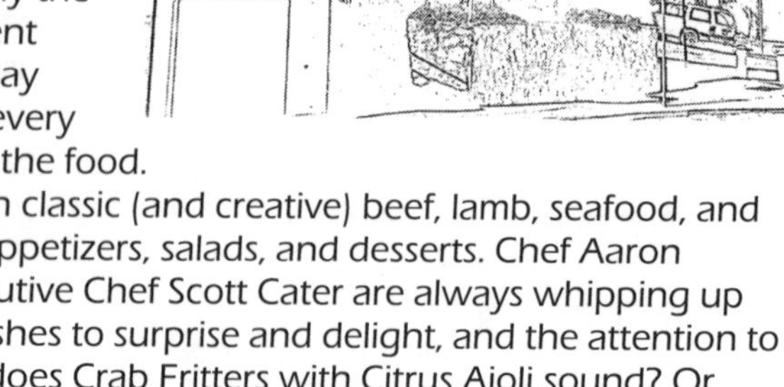

It's first-class dining with classic (and creative) beef, lamb, seafood, and pasta dishes. Yummy appetizers, salads, and desserts. Chef Aaron Cunningham and Executive Chef Scott Cater are always whipping up sumptuous seasonal dishes to surprise and delight, and the attention to detail is obvious. How does Crab Fritters with Citrus Aioli sound? Or perhaps Lamb Chops with Sesame Roasted Potatoes and Asian Plum Demi-Glace?

Check it out. It's one of those places you've probably walked by a thousand times without realizing the gem upstairs.

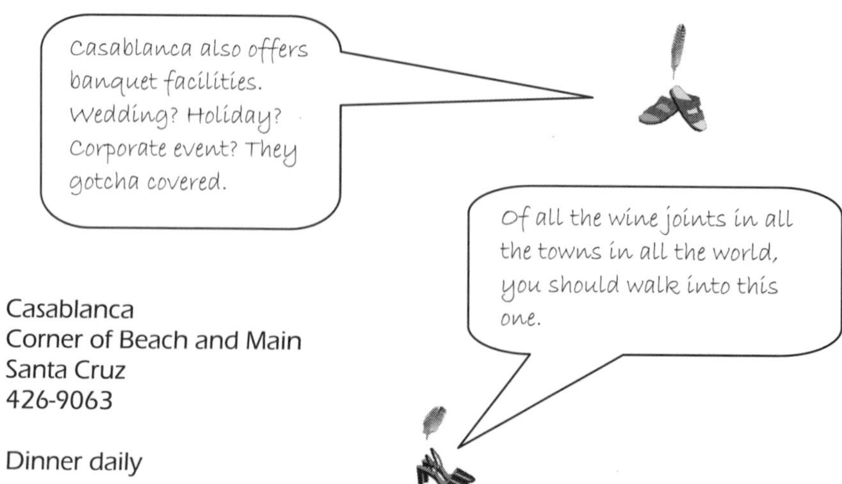

Casablanca also offers banquet facilities. Wedding? Holiday? Corporate event? They gotcha covered.
Of all the wine joints in all the towns in all the world, you should walk into this one.

Casablanca
Corner of Beach and Main
Santa Cruz
426-9063

Dinner daily

Casablanca's

Papaya Seed Vinaigrette

Ingredients

1 ripe papaya
3/4 C rice wine vinegar
juice from 1 lime
2 T honey
2-3 C canola oil
1 t salt

Preparation

- ✓ Peel the papaya and cut in half.
- ✓ Set aside the seeds from one of the halves; discard the remaining seeds.
- ✓ Cut the papaya into cubes and place in blender.
- ✓ Puree the papaya, vinegar, honey, and lime juice.
- ✓ When the puree is nice and smooth, slowly drizzle in oil until the dressing is a nice, creamy texture.
- ✓ Add the papaya seeds and salt. Puree until the seeds are well incorporated.
  The dressing should have a nice yellow/orange color with black speckles.

  If the dressing gets too thick when adding oil, adjust the consistency by adding some room-temperature water while the blender is on.

This dressing is great with fruit salad or mixed greens. In Hawaii, it is traditionally used with shredded green (unripe) papaya to make a condiment for pork.

Ciao Bella

When you walk into Ciao Bella, you pass right over a ruby-slippered witch, who is tragically trapped under the porch of this mountain-house-turned-eating-establishment. At this point, strange things happen: the lyrics to Jefferson Airplane's *White Rabbit* run through your mind; you begin to think that Ben Lomond is actually a portal to a parallel (and decidedly punk) universe; the whole world seems slightly tilted. The wait-staff bursts into song and dance as you are seated, and the décor screams of early modern madness. Your senses are overloaded... and you want to turn and run for the serenity of The Olive Garden.

Then suddenly you are swept up in the enthusiasm of the staff, and you give into your altered state—you realize that this is an experience not to be missed. This is Ciao Bella, where anything goes. And we mean anything. Owner and performer Tad Morgan has taken the phrase "dining experience" to a whole new level, putting as much energy into the atmosphere at Ciao Bella as into its fabulous Italian food. Did we say atmosphere? More like a force-5 tornado.

But don't be fooled into thinking Ciao Bella is all flash and no pan. The food alone is worth the drive up the mountain. Terrific Italian fare with lots of fresh ingredients, skillfully prepared. What's more, you will be blown away by the portions and the low prices. This is one establishment that believes in dazzling its customers.

(And if you're wondering... it takes about an hour and half to return to your normal Olive-Garden sensibilities.)

Oh, and be sure you call for reservations.

Ciao Bella
9217 Highway 9
Ben Lomond
336-9221

Dinner nightly
Limited parking.

Ciao Bella's

Pollo Fettuccine Ciao Bella

Ingredients

5 chicken strips
2 oz prosciutto
1/2 T garlic
10 oz marinara sauce
8 oz fettuccine noodles

Preparation

- ✓ Sauté chicken strips in olive oil.
- ✓ Add prosciutto.
- ✓ After 2-3 minutes, add marinara sauce.
- ✓ When sauce boils, add the fettuccine noodles.

Clouds

I could go on and on about Clouds, but that really isn't necessary. Suffice it to say that I chose Clouds for my 50th-birthday lunch. After all, it was a momentous occasion, and I wanted a restaurant with fabulous food, amusing waiters, and an ambience that lets your breathe. Clouds did not disappoint. My friends and I enjoyed a delightful meal, and we toasted our advancing age well into the afternoon, unhurried by our charming waiter. Clouds has an easy elegance and genuine class—nothing pompous or stuffy—the kind of place where you let out a big *ahhhh* as you are seated. It is simply one of the most inviting restaurants around.

The food at Clouds is terrific—just check out the recipes that owner Lou Caviglia and Chef Todd Parfitt were willing to share— with surprising combinations of ingredients and gorgeous presentation. And if you like martinis, well, Clouds is your place. Even James Bond might be persuaded to try something new.

Clouds is a class act for lunch and dinner. You'll love the contemporary saloon atmosphere, the martinis, and especially the food.

As for Lou... well, you'll love his sense of humor. (Tell him we said Hi.)

You won't believe this Stuffed Mission Fig recipe—one of the most fantastic treats ever! I served these at a party, and they nearly caused a stampede.

Lou somehow made time to coach my daughter's softball team.

Clouds Downtown
110 Church Street
Santa Cruz
429-2000
www.cloudsdowntown.com

Lunch and dinner daily

Clouds'

Stuffed Mission Figs

with Port-Balsamic Reduction

Ingredients

a basket of figs
1/2 lb parma prosciutto, sliced thin
1 C cream cheese
1/8 cup sliced roasted almonds
1 t black pepper
1 T parsley, chopped
1 T chives, chopped

Preparation

- ✓ Cut figs in half (but not all the way through).
- ✓ Whip together the remainder of ingredients(except the prosciutto), by hand or in a Kitchenaide.
- ✓ Fill each fig with the cheese mixture.
- ✓ Wrap individual figs with prosciutto.
- ✓ Grill on hot grill until prosciutto is crispy.
- ✓ Place on plate and drizzle with Port-Balsamic Reduction (recipe follows).

Port-Balsamic Reduction

- ✓ Mix equal parts port and balsamic vinegar (about 1 C each) (You do not need to use expensive port, but good balsamic is recommended.)
- ✓ Reduce slowly over moderate heat until syrupy.

Chef Todd Parfitt explains that this dish is rather simple—the quantities are not necessarily steadfast so it can be made in your own style.

Clouds'

Pork Loin

with wild mushroom sauce
and cauliflower au gratin

Ingredients

3-4 lb pork loin
1 C olive oil
1 C red wine
1/2 C balsamic vinegar
1 onion, chopped
5 garlic cloves, minced
1 C Gorgonzola

Preparation

- ✓ Slice the pork loin into 3/4-inch medallions.
- ✓ Marinate the medallions in the olive oil, red wine, balsamic vinegar, onion, and garlic.
- ✓ Grill on a hot grill.
- ✓ Top with Gorgonzola just before removing.
- ✓ Serve with Wild Mushroom Sauce (recipe follows).

Wild Mushroom Sauce

Ingredients

1 cube butter
1/4 lb parma prosciutto, diced
1 C sliced wild mushrooms
I whole head garlic, roasted
1 bunch green onions
1/2 C white wine
1/2 C demi-glace

Preparation

- ✓ In clarified butter sauté the prosciutto, mushrooms, garlic, and onion.
- ✓ When the mushrooms and onions are cooked, add the wine and reduce.
- ✓ Add demi-glace and reduce.
- ✓ Finish with butter.

Clouds'

Cauliflower au Gratin

Ingredients

1/2 lb bacon
1 onion, chopped
5 cloves garlic, minced
1 C heavy cream
1 head cauliflower florets
1/4 C grated Parmesan cheese
1/4 C bread crumbs

Preparation

- ✓ Preheat oven to 350 °.
- ✓ Dice raw bacon and render over low heat.
- ✓ When bacon is cooked, add onion and garlic.
- ✓ Deglaze with white wine.
- ✓ When white wine is reduced, add cream and cauliflower.
- ✓ Cook until cauliflower is al dente.
- ✓ Remove from liquid and place in baking dish.
- ✓ Add enough cream mixture into baking dish to cover bottom of dish
- ✓ Top with Parmesan and bread crumbs.
- ✓ Bake until golden brown.

The Crepe Place

When you enjoy a delectable meal or dessert at The Crepe Place, keep in mind everything the owners have been through to keep their restaurant going. On Christmas Eve, 1988, a terrific storm blasted the shale cliff above their restaurant (then located near the Town Clock), sending tons of rock crashing down. (No one was hurt.) After 15 years, Gary and Marlene Keeley were suddenly out of business. As luck would have it, The Cooper House in downtown Santa Cruz had a new owner, who was looking for a new restaurant tenant. So the Keeleys joyously moved into their Cooper House location in June 1989 — four months before the devastating earthquake that destroyed most of downtown Santa Cruz. The Cooper House was red tagged, and the Keeleys weren't even allowed back in their restaurant. They lost all of their equipment and 90% of their antiques and artwork. (No one was hurt.) Amazingly, the Keeleys reopened The Crepe Place the following March in their current location. (Luckily, no one was hurt.)

While the Keeleys may be tough, fortunately their crepes are not. These delicate little "pancakes" can be filled with brie for an elegant appetizer or seasonal fruit for a fun dessert. They are also perfect for after- hours dining. In fact, The Crepe Place is the ideal spot for a late night, clandestine rendezvous — a touch of romance and intrigue.

But crepes are not the only pleasure to be had. The Crepe Place also serves fine house chowder, beautiful, fresh salads, home-made soups, some great vegetarian meals, and luscious desserts.

In France, it is the custom to prepare crêpes for La Chandeleur Candlemas (February 2nd), for they symbolize good crops, good health, and wealth for the upcoming year. In Santa Cruz, they also seem to symbolize resilience... and just plain old fun.

The Crepe Place has won awards for Best Late Night and Best Outdoor dining.

The Crepe Place
1134 Soquel Avenue
Santa Cruz
429-6994
www.thecrepeplace.com

I agree. I love their heated patio!

Lunch and dinner daily
Brunch Sat and Sun

The Crepe Place's

The Crepe Gatsby

Ingredients

For the crepes (makes 6)

1/3 C white flour
2/3 C whole wheat flour
1 T sugar
1 egg
1 C milk
1 T cooking oil

The crepe batter is best if made the day before.

For the filling

chicken breast, cubed (approximately 1/2 lb)
3 oz white cheddar, grated
sundried tomato pesto
1/2 bunch spinach, washed and chopped
3 oz mushrooms, sliced
6 scallions, sliced

Preparation

- ✓ Combine the flour, sugar, egg, and milk in a mixing bowl. Beat until smooth.
- ✓ Add the cooking oil to the batter; mix well.
- ✓ Heat a seasoned cast iron pan* until very hot.
- ✓ Ladle 1/3 C of the batter into the crepe pan.
- ✓ Cook until edges begin to curl, approximately one minute.
- ✓ Flip and cook the other side, approximately 30 seconds.
- ✓ Sprinkle crepe with 1/2 oz cheese and allow to melt.
- ✓ Add a proportionate amount of remaining ingredients.
- ✓ Fold crepe over and allow ingredients to cook down.
- ✓ Remove the crepe to a plate, brush with melted butter, and top with grated Romano cheese.

* The Crepe Place uses cast iron pans instead of traditional crepe pans.

Crow's Nest

Throw off the bowlines and sail into Santa Cruz's favorite meeting place for a friendly meal and magnificent view of the Monterey Bay—the Crow's Nest. Since its opening in1969 , the Crow's Nest has been a favorite destination for locals and tourists alike. With its stunning views and great food, the Crow's Nest has acquired a devoted following. And why not? The daily specials feature seafood brought in that same morning by the local fishing fleet. And the bountiful salad bar features locally grown produce. If you're not in the mood for seafood, Crow's Nest has an extensive menu that includes wonderfully aged steaks and pasta dishes.

In addition to al fresco dining, the Crow's Nest offers a safe harbor on blustery days. Its interior boasts nautical themes, warm woods, expansive windows, surf memorabilia, all of which make for a cozy escape from the elements. An ideal location to relax, socialize, and enjoy a superbly prepared meal and your favorite fine wine or cocktail—all the while watching the sailboats zip by.

Entertainment, dancing, and live comedy on selected nights make Crow's Nest the ultimate Santa Cruz experience. And what could be better than a walk on the beach after a lovely evening of food and entertainment? It's just right off the forward bow...

Barbara Driscoll, the Grand Pooh Bah of Geezer Chicks, says the Shrimp Stuffed Artichoke is her favorite dish in the entire world.

Crow's Nest
at the yacht harbor
2218 E Cliff Drive
Santa Cruz
476-4560

Don't miss the Crow's Nest salad bar. It's terrific.

Lunch and dinner daily
All-day dining in the upstairs Breakwater Grill

Crow's Nest's

Coffee Mousse

Ingredients

3 egg whites
3/4 C white sugar
1 oz instant coffee
1 1/2 t vanilla extract
1/4 t salt
2 C whipping cream
toasted almonds
cinnamon

Preparation

- ✓ Chill mixing bowl and wire whip in freezer for half an hour.
- ✓ Beat egg whites on high speed until well blended and slightly stiff or peaked.
- ✓ Add sugar, instant coffee, vanilla, and salt, blending thoroughly.
- ✓ Slowly add whipping cream, blending until soft peaks form. DO NOT OVERMIX.*
- ✓ Spoon mousse into stem glasses (about 4 oz per glass).
- ✓ Sprinkle with toasted almonds and a dash of cinnamon.

Keep mousse in freezer until half an hour before serving.

* Overmixing can make the mousse grainy.

Serves 6

Did you know?

A Saudi Arabian woman may divorce her husband if he refuses to give her coffee.

The world's costliest coffee is Kopi Luwak, which costs $130-$300 a pound. The coffee bean is found in the droppings of a marsupial that eats only the very finest coffee plants. Plantation workers track the critters and scoop up their precious droppings.

Ummm, nothing like the smell of coffee brewing!

When you are drinking coffee, you are actually drinking fruit juice. (A coffee "bean" isn't really a legume, but rather the pit of a fruit.)

According to Archives of General Medicine, coffee drinkers have sex more often than non-coffee drinkers.

Not necessarily...

In 16th century Turkey, anyone caught drinking coffee was put to death.

Crow's Nest's

Peach, Cherry, & Poblano Chili Chutney

Ingredients

4 C dried peaches, coarsely chopped
2 1/4 C cider vinegar
2 C brown sugar
1 1/2 C roasted poblano chiles
1 C dried sweet cherries or cranberries
1 C red onion, chopped
2 cinnamon sticks
2 1/2 t mustard seed
1/2 T salt

Preparation

- ✓ In a large rondo, combine cider vinegar and red onions and bring to a boil.
- ✓ Boil for 5 minutes.
- ✓ Add remaining ingredients and return to a boil.
- ✓ Reduce heat to low and cook until all ingredients are tender and reduced, about 1hour.
- ✓ All to cool.
- ✓ Discard cinnamon sticks.
- ✓ Serve or cover and chill.

This chutney is a great finishing touch for grilled lamb, pork, or chicken. It will keep up to one month in the refrigerator.

DeLaveaga Lodge

If you want to hit a culinary hole in one, drive up to DeLaveaga Lodge restaurant, located at the beautiful DeLaveaga golf course. Locals love to come here for a substantial "scramble," lots of variety, interesting specials, and always a friendly face! You'll find many of your fellow patrons don't even play golf—they just come for the food or drink and to laugh with owner George Vomvolakis. And that's what strikes you about this restaurant: laughter and people just enjoying themselves. This attitude comes from owners Jon Bei and his daughter Marci, who apply their attitude of "life is too short not to enjoy" to all they do. With tables overlooking the putting green and the 18th hole lake, a person can easily spend a pleasant afternoon or morning enjoying these links (be they of the golf or linguica variety).

If you have a hankering for some greens, order their large shrimp Louie. Or if you need the comfort of a hot roast beef sandwich (with mounded wedges of thinly sliced beef on a roll, real mashed potatoes and creamy brown gravy), this is the place to try.

Casual and comfortable with big portions—that's what the De Laveaga Lodge is all about.

Oh, and if they have a lamb special on the day you visit, be sure not to miss it.

I highly recommend their roast beef sandwich. It's the best in the county!

I love sitting out on the terrace, enjoying the lovely weather, and dining on my daily roughage. Great salads!

DeLaveaga Lodge
Upper De Laveaga Park
Santa Cruz, Ca. 95060
(831) 423-1600

Breakfast and lunch daily

DeLaveaga's

Braised Short Ribs

over Creamy Polenta

Ingredients

4 T olive oil
3 lbs short ribs
salt, pepper, chopped garlic (to coat the ribs)
1 1/2 C onion, chopped
1 C celery, chopped
1 C carrot, chopped
1 1/2 C canned stewed tomatoes
2 T chopped garlic
1 C Merlot wine
1/4 C red wine vinegar
2 T Worcestershire sauce
1/2 C ketchup
1 bay leaf
3 t black pepper
2 qt beef broth

If you like veggies, feel free to increase these quantities. The more, the better!

Preparation

- ✓ Heat oil in a large, heavy pot that can be covered and put in the oven.
- ✓ Season ribs with salt , pepper, and garlic, rubbing the spices in with your hands.
- ✓ When the pot is nearly smoking, add the ribs (being careful not to splash the oil), searing one side until brown, and then turning the ribs over for the other side to brown.
- ✓ When ribs have browned, add onions, celery, carrots. Allow them to sweat a few minutes.
- ✓ Add tomatoes ,chopped garlic , merlot, ketchup, vinegar, Worcestershire, bay leaf, and broth. Heat to a simmer.
- ✓ Cover and put in oven until ribs are very tender, about 2 1/2 hours
- ✓ Mix 4 T corn starch with enough water to make a thick paste.
- ✓ Gently add the paste to the short ribs, a little at a time, until desired thickness.
- ✓ Season with salt and pepper to taste.

Did you know?

There are two different cuts of beef short ribs. One is from the shoulder, which is cut into rectangular chunks of meat, generally 2 to3 inches long, and includes layers of fat, meat, bone, and connective tissue. The second is from the short plate (the underside of the chest), and generally includes five ribs. This cut is also known as plate short ribs or simply beef ribs.

Short ribs are very tough and require long cooking to soften them up. (No quick microwave cooking for these guys.)

The history of the rib cut isn't known. However, the use of the rib meat most likely comes from the fact that carnivorous humans wanted to use every part of the animal carcass.

And of course, they wanted an effective transport system for their fiery barbecue sauce!

DeLaveaga's

Creamy Polenta

Ingredients

2 C polenta
6 C water
2 C milk
2 t salt
1/4 C butter*
1/2 C Parmigiano- Reggiano cheese, grated

Preparation

- ✓ In a heavy sauce pan over high heat, bring the water and milk to a boil.
- ✓ Add salt and, while stirring continuously with a wooden spoon, gradually stir in polenta in a thin, steady stream until all is incorporated.
- ✓ Continuing to stir to keep lumps from forming, reduce heat until the polenta bubbles only occasionally.
- ✓ Continue stirring until thick, smooth, creamy — about 20-25 minutes.
- ✓ Remove from heat and add butter.

To serve

- ✓ Spoon polenta in large bowls.
- ✓ Place ribs on top.
- ✓ Ladle each bowl with gravy.

Serves 4

* Chef Marci Bei says you can use more butter, up to3/4 cup ... like her Noni used to. And how 'bout a couple of handfuls of grated cheese?

Gilda's

My father had been craving a shrimp Louie for several months. But shrimp Louie just wasn't on the menu at the nursing home, so my father finally announced, "I wanna go to Gilda's!" I made a few phone calls, got the family together, and we all headed out to the wharf. Dad asked, "You make reservations?" I assured him that Gilda knew we were coming. "Did you tell 'em we want shrimp Louie? Don't want them running out..." I had to laugh. As though Gilda's would ever run out of shrimp!

Gilda's is the place my father and I always went for shrimp Louie. Literally decades of huge shrimp Louies, mountains of French bread, and meandering conversation. In all these years, Gilda's hasn't changed. It still has the 50s coffee-shop look; still the same, consistently good seafood. Still the same owners—Gilda herself and her brother, Big Boy Stagnaro. And still the same classic Louie. There's nothing nouveau about this salad—it's just how I remember it from my childhood. Iceberg lettuce. Piles of shrimp. Gooey dressing.

That Louie at Gilda's was the last "restaurant" meal my father would have—he died a couple of months after our dinner out. And I'm glad that his final big night out was at Gilda's, devouring that Louie as though the shrimp would escape were he not quick enough.

If a salad can ever be more than the sum of its ingredients, this one is it. Delicious. And bursting with memories and nostalgia.

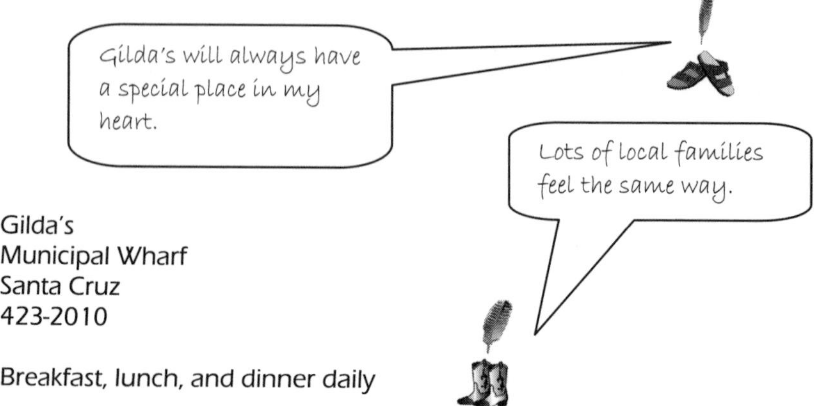

Gilda's will always have a special place in my heart.
Lots of local families feel the same way.

Gilda's
Municipal Wharf
Santa Cruz
423-2010

Breakfast, lunch, and dinner daily

Gilda's

Sautéed Prawns and Scallops

Ingredients

1/2 lb (15 large) prawns
1/2 lb (20-30) fresh Eastern scallops, hard muscle removed
1 T chopped garlic
1 T chopped shallots
1 T chopped parsley
2 T olive oil
6 oz vermouth, sauterne, or dry white wine
juice of one lemon (no seeds)
salt and pepper to taste
4-6 oz butter, cut into cubes and at room temperature

Preparation

- ✓ Peel and devein the prawns.
- ✓ Heat a large skillet until very hot.
- ✓ Add the olive oil, then the prawns and the scallops.
- ✓ Sauté until edges start to turn brown
- ✓ Add garlic and shallots and sauté until fragrant.
- ✓ Add the wine and the salt and pepper.
- ✓ Reduce wine by one half.
- ✓ When scallops are cooked through, add lemon juice and butter.
- ✓ Keep moving the butter with a spatula, scraping the bottom of the pan. (Do not let the butter separate. If it begins to separate, remove from heat.)
- ✓ When the butter has completely melted and emulsified (forming a sauce), add the parsley.
- ✓ Serve immediately with wild rice pilaf.

Serves 2-4

Tips:
A little wine can be added to stop the garlic and shallots from burning.
A Teflon or nonstick pan works best for this recipe. Also, it's helpful to cut the scallops to a thickness that matches the prawns.
And be sure the butter is room temp!

Green Valley Grill

Some of my fondest memories involve the Green Valley Grill. It was where my family gathered after my grandfather's funeral for a special meal and remembrance. And when my best friend, Rose, wanted to take me out to celebrate my 50th birthday, Green Valley Grill was my first and only choice. What attracts me to this restaurant? Besides the absolutely excellent food, it's the feeling I get when I'm there: I can savor my meal, unhurried in comfortable surroundings, while enjoying the pull of the Pajaro Valley, where my ancestors struggled as pioneers.

The oak wood grill cooks up local fare—delicious smoked ribs, chicken, and mouth-watering steaks. The smoke flavoring is a treat to the taste buds, and the experience is especially enhanced by the fresh, local grilled vegetables. I suggest you order the sampler GVG platter—it's the absolute best way to experience the specialties of the chef.

Green Valley Grill calls their cuisine "contemporary with traditional favorites." Let's just say I have never had a meal there I didn't love.

And don't be fooled by the entrance off the parking lot. It's just a short elevator ride to paradise. Hidden upstairs is a lovely restaurant, which is unassuming and dedicated to providing memorable meals to be shared with family and friends.

Full service bar; extensive wine list; banquet and private rooms available... who could ask for anything more?

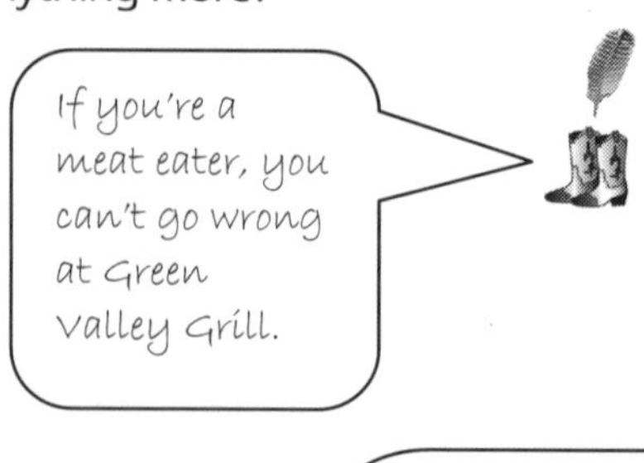

If you're a meat eater, you can't go wrong at Green Valley Grill.

Green Valley Grill
40 Penny Lane
Watsonville
728-0644

The Potatoes au Gratin is their most requested recipe. So here it is... for your dining pleasure.

Dinner Mon – Sat
Lunch Mon – Fri
Closed Sunday

Green Valley Grill's

Potatoes Au Gratin

Ingredients

9 large baking potatoes
1 1/2 C heavy cream
3/4 lb Monterey Jack cheese, grated
2 t salt
pepper

Preparation

- ✓ Bake potatoes at 450° until soft (about 45 minutes).
- ✓ Cool 10 minutes. (Do not let potatoes cool completely.)
- ✓ Cut each potato in half lengthwise.
- ✓ Scoop out all of the potato flesh and place it in a 9 X 12 baking pan.
- ✓ Sprinkle on salt.
- ✓ Top with grated cheese.
- ✓ Pour cream over the top.
- ✓ Sprinkle with pepper (to taste).
- ✓ Back at 450° until top is golden brown (about 15 minutes).

Serves 7-9

Harbor Café

A popular hang out for locals is the Harbor Café. Located up from the Yacht Harbor, this restaurant is low key, catering to the unique Santa Cruz style. The older building with its eclectic garden patio and funky decorations just makes you happy and relaxed. No one will think twice about that T shirt and shorts you're wearing.

There is nothing more "Santa Cruz" than sitting on the outside patio, reading the Sentinel, sipping really good coffee out of heavy stoneware mugs, while catching up on the news. We always get one of the eggs benedict dishes, which is especially enjoyable in the warm coastal sun.

The Harbor Café serves breakfast, lunch, and dinner, with all meals offering lots of interesting choices: fish tacos (for which Harbor Café is famous), calamari, vegetarian meals, mesquite grilled meats, organic salads and fresh seafood. The white stoneware dishes and heavy flatware remind me of old-fashioned home cooking, and the continuous coffee fill-ups make me remember that good service is an art.

I think of the Harbor Café as a wonderful place to unwind. A wide (and interesting) variety of fresh food. Great coffee. Friendly staff. All in all, a veritable sanctuary from our fast-paced world. No worries, be happy!

I love sitting out on a Sunday afternoon, Baxter at my feet, a mug of coffee in hand...

Harbor Café
535 7th Avenue
Santa Cruz
475-0213

The staff at the Harbor Café invite you to come on over and give their San Felipe Tacos the ultimate taste test. Or you can make them yourself using this recipe.

Breakfast and lunch Thurs – Mon
Dinner Fri and Sat

Harbor Café's

San Felipe Tacos

Ingredients

Snapper (any white, flaky fish will work)
2 corn tortillas
1/2 green cabbage, thinly sliced
1 tomato, diced
1/2 bunch cilantro

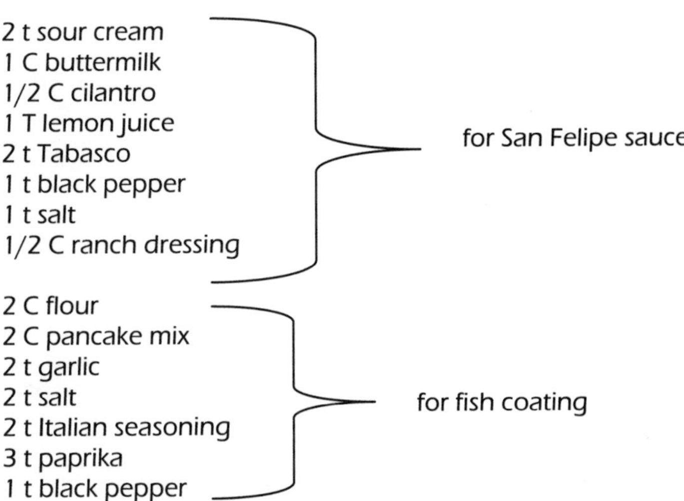

For San Felipe sauce:

2 t sour cream
1 C buttermilk
1/2 C cilantro
1 T lemon juice
2 t Tabasco
1 t black pepper
1 t salt
1/2 C ranch dressing

For fish coating:

2 C flour
2 C pancake mix
2 t garlic
2 t salt
2 t Italian seasoning
3 t paprika
1 t black pepper

Preparation

- ✓ Mix the cabbage, diced tomato, and 1/2 bunch of cilantro in a bowl and set aside.
- ✓ Mix together the ingredients for fish coating.
- ✓ Lightly bread the snapper in the coating.
- ✓ Fry the fish until it's a beautiful golden color.
- ✓ Place the fish on warmed tortillas.
- ✓ Top with fresh slaw.
- ✓ Top with San Felipe sauce.

Hindquarter Bar and Grille

When the owners of the Hindquarter Bar and Grille claim their restaurant is "where the elite meat," they aren't kidding. It's all about MEAT at this dining establishment— prime rib, Texas T-bones, smoked ribs, ... It's an Atkin's Nirvana.

Of course, the Hindquarter also serves up free-range chicken, grilled to perfection, as well as fresh, locally caught seafood. And the Hindquarter even offers an impressive vegetarian menu. (The restaurant's located in Santa Cruz after all!) But let's face it: this is the place where carnivores roam freely and unapologetically.

Owners Bob and Sandy Cornell have been asking, "What's your beef?" for 16 years now. And Sandy, like the seafood and produce she serves, is locally grown and extremely fresh. (An actual Santa Cruz native!)

The menu at Hindquarter seems to go on forever—not the best of situations for someone who is indecisive. So you may end up like me, with my one or two favorites, or (if you're really lucky), you'll end up like my friend, Emily, who always tries something new. "Well, there's the Calamari Steak Piccata.... or the Smokey Platter sounds good...." While she's making up her mind, I'm fantasizing about a big, juicy filet mignon. And at Hindquarter, my dreams always come true.

The Good Times has given the Hindquarter its Best Steakhouse award 15 years running.

Hindquarter Bar & Grille
303 Soquel Avenue
Santa Cruz, California
426-7770
www.thehindquarter.com

Dinner daily
Lunch Mon –Sat

This recipe is one of the most popular Specials at the Hindquarter. Even though it's not on the regular menu, it's a favorite among regulars.

Hindquarter's

North Beach Rib Eye Steak

Ingredients

4 11- or 12-oz boneless rib-eye steaks
6-8 garlic cloves
olive oil
4 oz Gorgonzola cheese
2 oz soft butter
2 sprigs fresh rosemary
whole black peppercorns

Preparation

- ✓ Heat oven to 300°.
- ✓ Place garlic cloves in a small glass baking dish and cover with olive oil. Bake for 45 minutes, stirring occasionally, until golden brown.
- ✓ Finely chop rosemary leaves.
- ✓ Place the garlic, Gorgonzola cheese, butter, rosemary, and 1 t of olive oil in food processor and pulse until coarsely blended.
- ✓ Carefully cut a horizontal slit in the side of each rib-eye steak from the bone side to form a pocket in the eye of the steak.
- ✓ Fill each pocket with 1 1/2 T of the cheese mixture.
- ✓ Close pockets with toothpicks.
- ✓ With the flat side of a large chef's knife, coarsely crush enough peppercorns to make 1/4 C. Sprinkle 1/2 T on each side of each steak (or to taste) and press in lightly.
- ✓ Season to taste with salt.
- ✓ Grill steaks over hot charcoal to desired doneness.
- ✓ Garnish each steak with 1 t of the cheese mixture and a rosemary sprig.
- ✓ Remove toothpicks and enjoy!

Serves 4

Ideal Bar & Grill

Ideal Bar and Grill is located at the entrance to the Santa Cruz Municipal Wharf, making it an *ideal* location for anyone who wants to enjoy great food while people watching. With a great view of the beach and wharf, it's a natural spot for watching the world go by. The outdoor deck, in fact, offers the "best seats in town" when Santa Cruz hosts professional volleyball tournaments, such as the Jose Cuervo Open.

Of course, Ideal isn't packed on the weekends just because of its location. Its food is also *ideal*, with an impressive selection of fresh produce, local seafood, steak, pasta, and vegetarian dishes. The menu is varied, and the Specials board is always worth a look.

The tourists who come to Santa Cruz may flock to Ideal on the weekends, but the locals know to take advantage of Ideal's weekday specials. For example, Wednesdays are Lobster Night and Fridays are Prime Rib night. The food is terrific, and you won't find a better value anywhere.

As if the beachfront location weren't enough, Ideal has live music every night during the spring and summer, and three nights a week during the off season. And their espresso bar opens every morning at 7 AM. Now that's what I call ideal!

Their lobster special is exceptional.
I had my most memorable New Year's Eve dinner here at Ideal.

Ideal Bar and Grill
106 Beach Street
Santa Cruz, Ca.
423-5271

Open daily from 7 AM

Ideal's

Artichoke Crusted Halibut

with Mint Vinaigrette

Ingredients

For the crust

2 16-oz cans artichoke crowns, drained
1 t chopped thyme
1 t chopped garlic
1/4 C buttermilk
1 T Dijon mustard
1/4 C fresh sourdough bread crumbs
1 t kosher salt
1/2 t fresh ground pepper
1 T lemon juice

For the fish

6 8-oz halibut filets
4 oz Asiago cheese, grated
2 T chopped parsley
1 T olive oil
1 T fresh lemon juice
1 16-oz can artichoke bottoms

Preparation

- ✓ Preheat oven to 350°.
- ✓ In a food processor, grind all of the crust ingredients.
- ✓ Season fish with salt and pepper.
- ✓ Coat each fish filet with a 1/4-inch layer of crust.
- ✓ Top each filet with Asiago cheese.
- ✓ Slice the remaining artichoke bottoms into 1/4-in slices, placing one slice on each filet.
- ✓ Drizzle olive oil and lemon juice over each filet.
- ✓ Bake for approximately 10 minutes.
- ✓ Top with mint vinaigrette. (Recipe follows.)

Did you know?

Halibut live on the bottom of the ocean floor off Alaska's coast and can weigh over 400 pounds.

Two submarines of the United States Navy have been named the USS Halibut.

The Pacific halibut (*Hippoglossus stenolepis*) was called "haly-butte" in Middle English, meaning the flatfish that's to be eaten on Holy Days.

Halibut live quite a long time. The oldest recorded female was 42 years old and the oldest male was 27 years old.

Once again, the males poop out just when the females are hitting their stride.

When it comes to the Pacific halibut, the male and female both lays eggs.

Ideal's

Mint Vinaigrette

Ingredients

2 medium tomatoes, diced
2 shallots, diced
1/4 C mint, chopped
1/4 C lemon juice
1 t kosher salt
1/2 t fresh ground pepper
2 T sherry vinegar
1/4 C olive oil

Preparation

- ✓ Mix all of the ingredients together in a bowl.
- ✓ Chill for at least one hour before serving.

Ironwood's

I'm always happy to point out to tourists that the California redwood (Sequoia Sempervirens) is the tallest tree in the world. "You **have** to see the trees in Big Basin," I'll insist. And they usually counter with, "Well, how far is it?" (as though the tallest trees in the world should be visible from Santa Cruz). Luckily, I can promise much more than an eyeful of redwood— because along the road to Big Basin State Park is the Boulder Creek Golf & Country Club. To an out-of-towner, it's a little shocking to come around a tight turn on a narrow mountain road and see, of all things, a golf course and resort. But there it is—ready to accommodate the hungry, weary Sempervirens seeker. The golf course is breathtaking, even for those of us who don't golf. And Ironwood's restaurant, overlooking the first fairway, provides a perfect spot for soaking in the scenery and soaking up some great local fare.

Ironwood's is a quaint establishment with a decidedly mountain feel to it. Lots of wood. A cozy fireplace. A relaxed atmosphere. Executive Chef Ken Blake and Chef Chris Mack offer a fabulous continental-style cuisine, such as the recipe that follows, as well as a wonderful selection of local wines. So if you happen to be passing through Boulder Creek, or you're on your way to Big Basin State Park, be sure to give Ironwood's a try.

And if you're touring on a Sunday morning, check out Ironwood's Sunday brunch. It's one of the best around!

Ironwood's
Boulder Creek Golf & Country Club
16901 Big Basin Highway
Boulder Creek
338-2111

Breakfast and lunch daily
Dinner Fri – Mon
Brunch Sun

This is one place that consistently shoots above par.

Ironwood's

Pan-Seared Scallops

Ingredients

2 T Butter
6 large sea scallops
seasoned flour (1 C. all-purpose flour, 1 t garlic powder, 1 t black pepper, 1/2 t salt)
6 medium mushrooms (sliced)
3 slices bacon, pre-cooked and coarsely chopped
2 green onions, chopped
1t minced garlic in oil
1 pinch white Pepper
1 pinch salt
2 oz lemon Juice
3 oz white Wine
3 oz chicken stock
3 oz heavy cream

Preparation

- ✓ Dredge (dust) the scallops in the seasoned flour.
- ✓ In a medium skillet, melt 1 T butter over medium-high heat.
- ✓ When the butter is bubbling and quite hot, gently brown the scallops on both sides.
- ✓ Remove the scallops and set aside.
- ✓ In a fresh skillet, melt the remaining butter over medium to low heat.
- ✓ Add the mushrooms, bacon, green onions and spices.
- ✓ When the mushrooms have absorbed most of the butter, add the lemon juice and reduce by half.
- ✓ Add the wine and reduce by half.
- ✓ Add the chicken stock and reduce by half.
- ✓ Add the cream and reduce by half.
- ✓ Arrange the scallops on the plate and pour the finished sauce over them. (Sauce should be thick enough to coat the back of a spoon.)
- ✓ Serve immediately.

Serves 1

La Bruschetta

La Bruschetta is in the beautiful old Felton Guild, surrounded by majestic redwoods and massive oaks. Over the years, several restaurants have come and gone in this location, but it appears La Bruschetta is a keeper. And I could not be happier. This is an absolutely wonderful restaurant!

The dining room is airy and welcoming, but most of the year you'll likely opt to eat in the beautiful courtyard. It is no surprise that many people choose La Bruschetta for their wedding. The courtyard and adjoining lush lawns make it the perfect backdrop for any festive gathering of family and friends — they can accommodate parties of 250+! — and who better to cater a special occasion than the talented chef/proprietor, Luca Rubino!

I just have to tell ya... I love this restaurant. I love this food. And then there's Luca! This is the man every passionate, creative (and, truth be told, adorable) Italian chef is modeled after. He's the guy in every Fellini movie that all the women want to either mother or marry, and that all the men simply wish they could be. He cooks from his heart, not an index card...which made providing this recipe a little tricky. While Luca cooked, his restaurant manager, Ryan, measured ingredients, took notes, and did his best to capture Luca's instincts. So when you see his recipe calls for a handful of this and a little of that, relax. Luca has shared one of his special recipes and invites you to make it your own. Taste, smell, experiment, listen to that little Italian chef inside of you and, most of all, enjoy.

Good food, good fun, good friends. La Bruschetta is a Geezer Chicks kinda place. La dolce vita!

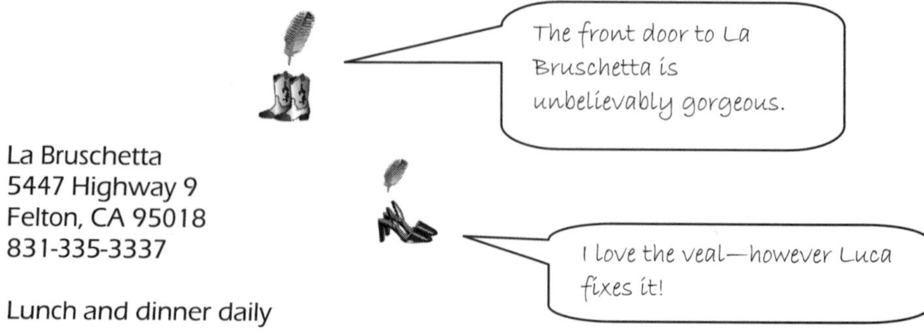

The front door to La Bruschetta is unbelievably gorgeous.
I love the veal—however Luca fixes it!

La Bruschetta
5447 Highway 9
Felton, CA 95018
831-335-3337

Lunch and dinner daily

La Bruschetta's

Involtini di Pesce Spada

Ingredients

4 lbs swordfish
6 T olive oil
1 yellow onion, chopped
1 handful raisins (golden or regular)
1 handful olives, halved
1 handful of pine nuts
1 handful of sundried tomatoes, chopped
1 bunch Italian parsley, chopped
3 cloves garlic, chopped
splash of white wine
juice of 1 lemon
pinch of salt and pepper

Preparation

- ✓ Mix freshly squeezed lemon juice, 4 T extra virgin olive oil, garlic, and parsley. Set aside.
- ✓ In a pan, warm 2 T olive oil over medium-hot flame.
- ✓ Sauté onion and garlic until onion starts to turn golden brown.
- ✓ Add a splash of wine, then add sundried tomatoes, pine nuts, olives, raisins, and a pinch of salt and pepper. (Reduce if necessary.)
- ✓ Allow ingredients to cool.
- ✓ Slice swordfish to 1/8-inch thickness.
- ✓ Place plastic wrap over and under the swordfish and hammer as thin as possible with a meat tenderizer.
- ✓ Place cooled ingredients on each slice of swordfish. (Do not overfill.)
- ✓ Roll each slice of fish like a burrito.
- ✓ Grill over medium flame to desired doneness. If grill is not available, bake in a preheated 350° oven for approximately 10 minutes.
- ✓ Top with salt and pepper and dressing (from first step).
- ✓ Serve immediately.

Serves 4-6

Did you know?

Offshore species of swordfish can be found worldwide in temperate and tropic waters. They are known to frequent depths of 400 to 500 fathoms, but also have been found basking at the surface of the ocean.

Swordfish feed mainly at night on squid, herring, mackerel, tuna, and other fish. They slash their prey with their sword-like bills. (Touché!)

Swordfish can live longer than 25 years and can weigh up to 1,200 pounds. At the turn of the century, however, the average swordfish landed weighed 300 to 400 pounds. In 1963, the average fish landed weighed 266 pounds. In 1996, the average fish weighed 90 pounds.

Florida's record swordfish catch was 612 lbs.,12 ozs.

Large swordfish are all females. Males seldom exceed 200 pounds.

La Bruschetta's

Bruschetta Salmonata

Ingredients

1/2 loaf bread (baguette)
150 grams (approx 4 oz) filet of smoked salmon
250 grams (approx 8 oz) Mascarpone cheese
100 grams(approx 3 1/2 oz) Gorgonzola
1/2 oz heavy whipping cream
walnuts (optional)
A little bit of chopped parsley

Preparation

- ✓ Slice bread and toast (preferable on a grill).
- ✓ Using a fork, mix the Gorgonzola and the Mascarpone with the cream until it is homogenous.
- ✓ Break up the smoked salmon and add to the mixture.
- ✓ Top the sliced bread with the mixture.
- ✓ Top with crushed walnuts, if desired.
- ✓ Garnish with parsley.

Serves 6

Michael's on Main

Chef/owner Michael Clark calls his style "cutting edge comfort cuisine." From my experience, this means some of my perennial favorites made just a bit better, incorporating Corralitos meats and locally produced wines, cheeses, and organic veggies. Food like (you wish) your mama made. And what a fun eclectic restaurant this is! The oak-shrouded creekside deck, illuminated by candles and twinkle lights, makes for a charming dinner setting (with heaters keeping it toasty year 'round); by day, it overlooks the flower and herb garden and...uh...oh yeah, the creek.

Two main dining rooms (one with a fireplace) showcase the work of local artists and can be readily transformed from funky to formal. The full bar is in one corner of the ideal Santa Cruz-style great room—high ceiling, lots of window, an inviting massive stone fireplace and comfy seating. Michael's describes its tiny wine cellar room as Victorian inspired. (I was reminded of a secret underground *DaVinci Code* room...and can't wait for an excuse to reserve this unique spot for a small meeting or party.) In fact, any or all of Michael's rooms, creekside deck and front courtyard, can be reserved for parties, weddings, meetings or other events.

But Michael's on Main offers more than a beautiful setting and great food. There's also weekday happy hour, karaoke night, special food and wine pairings, Sunday brunch, live music and open mic nights—even dinner theater. With its extended hours and convenient location right off Highway 1, Michael's on Main is the ideal place for a relaxed feel-good meal.

Michael is an expert at pairing just the right wine with just the right food.
I understand Brussels sprouts are back by popular demand. Can it be?

Michael's on Main
2591 Main Street
Soquel, CA 95073
831-479-9777

Lunch and dinner Tues – Sun

Michael's on Main's

Potato Bravo Farms Sharp Cheddar Torta

Ingredients

2 1/2 lb red potatoes
4 yellow onions, peeled and halved
2-3 T minced garlic
2 lb Bravo Farms sharp cheddar cheese
5 eggs
3 C cream
1/4 lb butter
1 T fresh thyme, minced
3 T fresh chives, minced
salt and pepper to taste

Preparation

- ✓ Preheat oven to 325
- ✓ Butter and line an 8" spring-form pan with parchment paper.
- ✓ Lightly butter the paper.
- ✓ Using a food processor, thinly slice the potatoes and the onion. (The slices should be paper thin.)
- ✓ Sauté sliced onions and garlic in butter until golden brown.
- ✓ In prepared spring-form pan, arrange one-fourth of the sliced potatoes in a flower petal design.
- ✓ Sprinkle with 1/3 of the cheese, 1/3 of the onion mixture, and a sprinkling of thyme and chives.
- ✓ Repeat the layers two more times.
- ✓ Finish with a top layer of potato slices, arranged in a petal design.
- ✓ In a mixing bowl, beat the eggs until smooth and consistent; beat in the cream to make a custard.
- ✓ Add salt and pepper.
- ✓ Pour custard over potatoes.
- ✓ Place spring-form pan in oven on top of a cookie sheet and bake for 1 – 1 1/4 hours, or until an inserted knife comes out clean.
- ✓ Serve with sour cream and garnish with chopped chives.

Serves 6-8

May be served hot or at room temp.

Did you know?

The artichoke was most likely cultivated first in Sicily, Italy. The plant is mentioned in Greek and Roman literature as far back as 77AD.

Artichokes were cultivated by the North African Moors near Granada, Spain around 800AD. The artichoke made it to England in about 1548, but was not well received. (Perhaps they tried to eat it whole.)

The Spanish settlers brought artichokes to California in the 1600's. They did not become widely grown or used in California until the 1920's, when a local landowner decided to lease land previously dedicated to the growing of sugar beets to farmers willing to try this new and weird vegetable. His reasons were economic—artichokes were fetching high prices and farmers could pay triple what the sugar company did for the same land. By 1929, the artichoke was the third largest cash crop in Salinas Valley. (The price of mayonnaise rose as well.)

Castroville, California celebrates an Artichoke Festival each year in the spring.

Castroville and the artichoke really made it on the map when Marilyn Monroe was crowned Artichoke Queen in 1948.

Michael's on Main's

Artichoke Fall Press

Ingredients

1 C fresh basil leaves
1/3 C olive oil
2 T grated Bravo Farms sharp cheddar cheese
1 T drained capers
1 T white wine vinegar
2 t mustard
1 clove garlic

1 lb French bread round
12 oz canned artichoke hearts, drained and sliced
4 oz queso de oro, sliced
l medium tomato, sliced
2 C fresh spinach leaves, torn

Preparation

- ✓ Process first seven ingredients in a blender until nearly smooth.
- ✓ Cut top off of the French roll and hollow out each half.
- ✓ Leave a 1-ince shell.
- ✓ Spread the mixture over the two halves.
- ✓ On the bottom half, layer:
  half of the artichokes
  half of the queso de oro
  half of the tomatoes
  half of the spinach
- ✓ Repeat the layers.
- ✓ Place the top half of the bread on and press.
- ✓ Wrap lightly in saran wrap.
- ✓ Chill for 6-8 hours.
- ✓ Slice like a pie.

Serves 4-6

You can vary this recipe using different cheeses, albacore, smoked meats, herbs, or olives!

Miramar

When I was a kid, the Miramar was THE classy restaurant in town. It's where your parents went on that special anniversary. It's where Santa Cruz's elite ate on a regular basis. And it's where you'd have dinner on prom night—**if** your date had an ounce of class.

The Miramar of my memories was richly decorated, dark, formal, somewhat intimidating. But that certainly isn't the Miramar of today. The sunny, casual dining room makes you feel immediately welcome. And the outdoor patio is comfortable, friendly—with a breathtaking view of Monterey Bay. One thing that hasn't changed, however, is the outstanding food. Miramar has been cooking up fabulous seafood, steaks, and pasta since 1945. Now with all that practice, it's little wonder that Miramar continues to be a Santa Cruz landmark.

You'll find some of the more traditional dishes, such as seafood Louies and Miramar's Seafood Pot. But you'll also find dishes that didn't exist in the 40s, such as Grilled Cod Salsa Fresca. Traditional or nouvelle, Miramar has it all. With a fantastic view to boot.

Next time you're out on the Municipal Wharf, be sure to give Miramar a try. Whether a great dinner or appetizers and happy-hour specials in the full bar, you'll be sampling more than local fare—you'll be sampling local history.

(And if you happen to be seated near a teenage girl wearing a puce prom dress, please don't point and laugh.)

Eating at Miramar is like eating at Fisherman's Wharf in San Francisco.

Miramar Fish Grotto
Municipal Wharf
Santa Cruz
423-4441

Dinner and lunch daily
Brunch Sunday

Only you get to look out at a lighthouse instead of a prison!

Miramar's

Ginger Scallops

Ingredients

1 C sugar
1 T ground ginger
2 C fresh orange juice
2 oranges
1 C fish stock
2 T cornstarch
1/2 C water
pinch of salt
2 T butter
1 lb fresh sea scallops
pickled ginger
sesame seeds
green onion, finely diced

Preparation

For the orange ginger sauce

- ✓ Zest the oranges. Finely dice the zest and set aside.
- ✓ Grate the oranges.
- ✓ Mix the sugar and the ground ginger.
- ✓ In a sauté pan, heat the sugar mixture, orange juice, grated orange, and fish stock. Reduce by half.
- ✓ Mix the water and cornstarch.
- ✓ Add the cornstarch mixture to the pan and cook until the sauce is clear and slightly thickened.
- ✓ Stir in the butter and pinch of salt.
- ✓ Gently simmer until the mixture is smooth.
- ✓ Add the orange zest.

For the scallops

- ✓ Grill the scallops 1-2 minutes per side.
- ✓ Place orange ginger sauce on a plate, place scallops on top of sauce.
- ✓ Garnish with pickled ginger, sesame seeds, and green onion.
- ✓ Serve with rice pilaf and fresh garden vegetable.

Serves 10

Ostrich Grill

I used to work right across from the Ostrich Grill—I mean it was literally only a few steps from my office door. That first year I put on 10 pounds. Now, the good folks at the Ostrich Grill will point out that ostrich meat is lean and nutritious, and that there are many items on the menu appropriate for the weight conscious. But they're overlooking the fact that I dined with coworkers who loved ordering exotic appetizers and decadent desserts. Sure, I always ordered a fabulous salad that was more than enough to satisfy... but invariably one of my friend would ask, "Would you like a bite?" A bite? ***A bite?*** I discovered the hard way that the food at Ostrich Grill is just too good for "a bite."

Okay, let's talk ostrich. It's the best reason of all for dining at the Ostrich Grill. The first time I tried it, I was expecting the ubiquitous chicken taste, but was pleasantly surprised to find that ostrich tastes more like beef. But a very light, delicate beef. It was unlike anything I'd ever had before—positively fabulous.

Chef Michael Knowles works his magic with ostrich, but also with steaks, chops, seafood, and filets. Prepared over an oak-fired grill, each entrée is perfectly prepared. And the side dishes are a special treat all on their own. And the desserts? Well, I won't even **go** there.

I have so many pleasant memories of the Ostrich Grill—many still on my hips. But don't let that stop you from trying this fabulous Capitola restaurant.

A wine snob of my acquaintance absolutely trusts their wine selections and recommendations. Now THAT's saying something.

Ostrich Grill
820 Bay Ave
Capitola
477-9182

Dinner nightly

Ostrich Grill's

Bacon-Wrapped Ostrich Tenderloin

with Vegetable Ragu

Ingredients

16 oz ostrich tenderloin
2 slices bacon
1 ear corn
9 cherry tomatoes
2 yellow or green patty pan squash
1 oz chopped Fines herbs
2 C cream
1 clove garlic
1 shallot
1 t Meyer lemon zest
1 t Kosher salt
1/2 t fresh ground white pepper
2 oz olive oil

Ostrich meat may be purchased at Corralitos Market, Deluxe Market, and New Leaf Market. Or log onto ostrichgrowers.com

Preparation

- ✓ Cut the corn off of the cob and set aside.
- ✓ Place cream and corn cob in a heavy-bottom sauce pan. Heat and then steep.
- ✓ Wrap ostrich loin in bacon, season with black pepper, and then set aside.
- ✓ Cut cherry tomatoes in half.
- ✓ Slice squash to 1/4 inch thickness.
- ✓ Chop garlic and shallots.
- ✓ In a cast iron pan or on a wood-burning grill, cook the ostrich about 6 minutes. Remove from heat and allow to rest.
- ✓ While meat is resting, heat the olive oil in a sauté pan. Add the garlic and shallots.
- ✓ As garlic and shallots start to turn brown, add the corn, lemon zest, and the corn cream. Reduce to half.
- ✓ Add squash, tomatoes, herbs, salt, and white pepper.
- ✓ Spoon the ragu onto the center of a plate.
- ✓ Slice ostrich into ten pieces, then lay on top of the ragu.

Serves 2

Palapas

The issue for me at Palapas is the salsa and chips. I sit down, start stuffing my face, and before I know it, I have no room left for anything else. I love great salsa! My solution is to prepare for Palapas by fasting for 12 hours, doing a quick round of Sweatin' to the Oldies, and wearing elastic-waist pants—all of which allow me to do the impossible: continue eating after a half-dozen bowls of salsa. It's worth the training. Palapas is known for their top-notch Mexican cuisine, especially their grilled Camarones de Golfo a la Parrilla. But wait! That too is an appetizer. The truth is, I ate at Palapas three times before I ever tried an entrée.

But you **must** give it your best shot. Palapas has fabulous seafood, unbelievable "traditional" dishes. Carne Asada? It's made with rib-eye steak. And the margaritas! There are so many different kinds that my friend Julie camped on their terrace for a week just so she could try them all. (Most patrons thought Julie was a piece of performance art, so she really wasn't in the way.)

Luckily for me, the kind of serious eating I indulge in at Palapas requires that I occasionally come up for air. During those brief respites, I take time to enjoy the ambience: I feel like I'm on a cruise. Every table overlooks the Monterey Bay, and with two outdoor dining areas, it's impossible to escape that tropical feeling. (Okay, the fog sometimes rolls in and dampens the tropical illusion, but then I just dive back undersalsa.)

Palapas offers freshly made sauces, local seafood and produce, homemade corn tortillas, and that amazing choice of tequilas.

Wait 'til you try this Chile Verde recipe. It's worth the effort. Of course, if you're feeling lazy, you can always head to Palapas and try the real thing.

Palapas
Seascape Village
Aptos
662-9000

Lunch and dinner daily

Palapas'

Chile Verde

(pork in green sauce)

Ingredients

3 T vegetable oil
1 1/4 lb pork shoulder, cut into 1 ½-inch cubes
1 onion, finely chopped
2 garlic cloves, crushed
1/2 t cumin
1 t salt
1 t sugar
2 fresh serrano chiles, chopped with seeds
1 pasilla chile, seeded and stemmed
2 C tomatillo sauce (recipe follows)
fresh cilantro

Preparation

- ✓ Heat oil in large, heavy sauce pan.
- ✓ Add pork cubes, cooking over high heat until brown.
- ✓ Lower heat to medium and add onion and garlic, sautéing until soft.
- ✓ Stir in cumin, serrano chiles, and pasilla chile.
- ✓ Cook for 2 more minutes.
- ✓ Add tomatillo sauce and simmer over medium heat for 35 minutes.
- ✓ Add reserved liquid (from tomatillo sauce recipe) as needed to maintain a medium-thick gravy consistency.
- ✓ Season with salt and sugar.
- ✓ Serve with tortillas and cilantro as garnish.

Serves 4

Did you know?

Spanish priests who established missions throughout California were concerned about the native people's passion for the chile. In their infinite wisdom, the priests concluded that chiles must be an aphrodisiac and subsequently warned against their use. Predictably, the popularity of the chile skyrocketed.

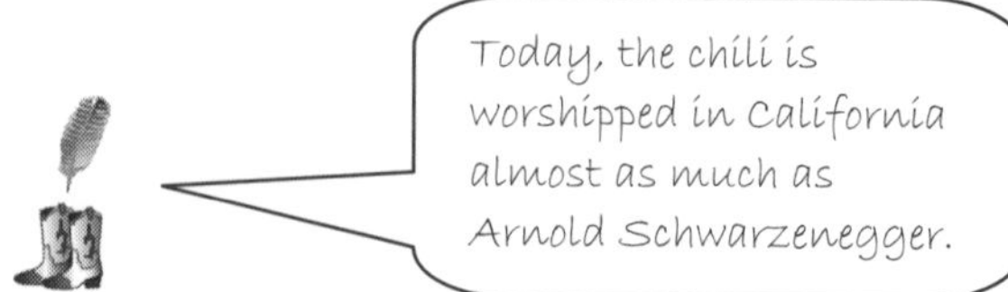

Today, the chili is worshipped in California almost as much as Arnold Schwarzenegger.

George Washington and Thomas Jefferson both grew chiles on their farms, although it's unclear whether they were fans of chips and salsa.

Are chilies addictive? Consider this. When capsaicin (the HOT in the chile) is ingested, it comes in contact with the nerves in your mouth and pain signals are sent to the brain. The brain then releases endorphins—you know, those natural painkillers— which create a feeling of well being. The spicier the food, the more endorphins released.

So... how many chiles would you like in your Tomatillo Sauce?

Tomatillo Sauce

Ingredients

20-25 tomatillos, husks removed
3 qt water
1 serrano chile, finely chopped
½ small onion, finely chopped
1 small clove garlic, finely chopped
1 t salt

Preparation

- ✓ Place tomatillos, onion, chile, and garlic into 3 quarts of water and bring to a boil.
- ✓ Maintain a moderate boil for 10-15 minutes, or until tomatillos begin to turn yellow.
- ✓ Strain tomatillo mixture, reserving liquid.
- ✓ Add salt to mixture and transfer to a blender.
- ✓ Blend mixture, adding enough reserved liquid to make a thin cream sauce.
- ✓ Strain sauce through medium strainer to remove seeds (which can be bitter).

If using this sauce for the Chile Verde recipe, be sure to reserve the liquid from the initial boiling.

Peachwood's Steakhouse

Although exquisite garden weddings are Peachwood's claim to fame, there is much more to Peachwood's than meets the I-Do.

Gracing the entrance to the Pasatiempo golf course, this Midwestern-style restaurant is known for its baby back ribs and steaks, which are cooked over actual peach wood. For diners in a less carnivorous mood, Peachwood's also offers a wide variety of fabulous salads and creative pasta dishes, all served in a friendly, comfortable setting. The menu is extensive, and not with its humor. The Chinese noodles and vegetable dish, for example, is called Wok on the Wild Side.

Peachwood's button-busting Sunday brunch is the stuff of legends—not to mention rapid weight gain. But not to worry! There's live music on the weekends, so you can dance off those calories.

Peachwood's is the perfect setting for casual dining, business meetings, family reunions, and (yes) weddings. Owner Dave Smith's philosophy of "having fun" imbues every aspect of the Peachwood's experience. What's more, Peachwood's is conveniently located right off Highway 17— and it's open 365 days a year! So just relax. And satisfy that craving for aged steak and ribs.

Check out the dining room with all the cuckoo clocks. It's a hoot at noon, when all the clocks go off at once.

Peachwood's Steakhouse
555 Highway 17
Santa Cruz
426-6333

Dinner daily
Lunch Mon – Sat
Brunch Sun

My friend had her wedding here, and the food and service were terrific.

Peachwood's

Castroville Artichoke Heart Cakes

Ingredients

2 12-ounce cans of artichoke hearts (drained)
1 celery stalk
1 small onion, chopped
1/4 green bell pepper, chopped
5 sprigs parsley, chopped
1/4 t cayenne pepper
1/4 t thyme
juice from one small lemon
2 C Italian bread crumbs

Preparation

- ✓ Mix all ingredients well and allow to stand for one hour. (This will help infuse the flavors.)
- ✓ Form into 3/4 inch-thick patties. (You should end up with about 15 patties.)
- ✓ Heat a small amount of olive oil in a skillet.
- ✓ Sauté the cakes until golden brown on both sides.
- ✓ Serve in a small pool of Light Lemon Beurre Blanc. (Recipe follows.)

Yields about 15 cakes

Did you know?

California is the largest producer of peaches. Most are grown in the San Joaquin Valley, just south of Fresno, California. In fact, California produces approximately 60 percent of all the peaches grown in the U.S. Believe it or not, South Carolina is a distant second in peach growing, with15 percent of the U.S. crop, and Georgia—Georgia!—comes in third with 13 percent of the total peach production.

There are over 200 varieties of peaches sold commercially from California—each with its own specific harvest time, flavor, and color characteristics.

The nectarine and the peach are so similar that only one gene separates the two, making them distinct. The nectarine has one recessive gene. Can you guess which one it is? The one with the fuzz!

How in the world do they know which gene is "the fuzz"?
The one with the badge.

Peachwood's

Light Lemon Beurre Blanc

Ingredients

2 T finely chopped shallots
1 T olive oil
1/2 C white wine
1/2 C white wine vinegar
2 C heavy cream
1 lb unsalted butter, cut into chunks
1 fresh lemon

Preparation

- ✓ Sauté the shallots in the olive oil. (Do not brown.)
- ✓ Add white wine and vinegar.
- ✓ Simmer until reduced to 1/4 cup.
- ✓ Add cream.
- ✓ Simmer until reduced to 2 cups.
- ✓ Transfer the mixture to a blender.
- ✓ Blending at low speed, add the butter, a little at a time.
- ✓ Add the juice of one lemon, the zest from one-quarter lemon, and salt and white pepper to taste.

Makes 1 quart

Peachwood's

Peach Soufflé

Ingredients

10 eggs
1/4 C flour
1 C sugar
1 C milk
1 T peach flavoring or vanilla
1/4 C unsalted butter
1 peach slice
1/8 t cream of tartar
1 t vanilla

Preparation

For the soufflé sauce

Be sure to reserve the egg whites for the soufflé below.

- ✓ Heat milk until hot. (Do not boil.)
- ✓ Separate 6 eggs.
- ✓ Combine yolks and 1/2 C sugar, mixing well.
- ✓ Add flour and flavoring, mixing well.
- ✓ SLOWLY add hot milk, a little at a time.
- ✓ Transfer mixture to stove and heat until thick. (Do not brown.)
- ✓ Set aside.

For the soufflé

- ✓ Separate the 4 remaining eggs. (Discard these egg whites or use for another purpose.)
- ✓ In a double boiler, blend egg yolks with 1/2 C sugar until a thick coating forms on the back of a spoon.
- ✓ Cool and add the vanilla.
- ✓ In a clean mixing bowl, combine the 6 egg whites (reserved from the sauce) with the cream of tartar.
- ✓ Using a wire-whip mixer at high speed, beat the egg whites until they form stiff peaks.

Putting it all together

- ✓ Preheat oven to 400°.
- ✓ Coat the inside of four soufflé cups with butter; add enough sugar and swirl so that the butter is completely coated with sugar. Tap out remaining sugar.
- ✓ Add half of the stiff egg white to the egg yolk mixture and mix until the color is blended.
- ✓ DO NOT OVERMIX.
- ✓ Fold in remaining egg whites
- ✓ Place a peach slice in the bottom of each cup.
- ✓ Add soufflé mixture until it is 1 inch over the top. Smooth the mixture with your finger to take off the excess.
- ✓ Place in oven for 8-15 minutes or until soufflé rises.
- ✓ Poke a spoon into the middle of each finished soufflé and pour in peach soufflé sauce.
- ✓ Sprinkle with powdered sugar.
- ✓ Serve immediately!

Serves 4

Ristorante Avanti

Okay, check out this unassuming restaurant front, located in a strip mall on Mission Street. Would you imagine that inside is one of Santa Cruz's best kept secrets? Well, I guess it's not **that** big of a secret, given that Ristorante Avanti tends to be packed every night of the week. And small wonder. Chef Brian Curry (love the name, by the way) sticks to seasonal dishes using organic, locally grown produce and the freshest of ingredients. Because Curry follows the seasonal offerings, the menu is constantly changing—with the exception of the baked meatballs, which is one of Ristorante Avanti's more popular dishes with locals.

Owners Paul and Cindy Geise emphasize FRESH in everything they do, right down to the mushrooms, which Paul hunts down and picks himself. (Don't worry. He knows what he's doing.) Even the bread is special—delivered fresh daily from Gayle's Bakery.

It's safe to say that, after18 years in the same location, Ristorante Avanti is here to stay. So why not give them a try? You'll get to sample the best in California-Italian cuisine, you'll be supporting local farmers in the process, and you'll come away feeling completely satisfied—**and** determined to keep the secret.

This bar is a favorite watering hole of Westside's The Young and the Nulliparous.

It's young, it's hip, it's loud... but they still serve Geezer Chicks. Like we needed another reason to love this spot...

1711 Mission Street
Santa Cruz
427-0135

Dinner daily
Lunch Mon – Fri

Ristorante Avanti's

Oven Roasted Tomato Sauce

Ingredients

7-10 lbs ripe tomatoes (Early Girl, Roma, San Marzano)
2-3 sweet onions (such as Cioppolini heirloom onions)
2 fennel bulbs
15-20 cloves garlic
2-3 bay leaves
springs of fresh basil and oregano (to your taste)
1/4 C sugar
salt
olive oil
1 bottle white wine

This recipe makes a lot of sauce — 4-5 quarts— so plan on freezing some for later use.

Preparation

- ✓ Preheat oven to 300°.
- ✓ Wash tomatoes and fennel.
- ✓ Cut tomatoes in half; thinly slice fennel and onions.
- ✓ Place the tomatoes, fennel, and onions in a large casserole or baking pan.
- ✓ Add garlic and sugar.
- ✓ Drizzle with olive oil to lightly coat.
- ✓ If using dried herbs instead of fresh, add them now.
- ✓ Season with salt.
- ✓ Bake in oven until juices release, then continue to bake until sauce is reduced by half. (Stir often.)
- ✓ Add white wine and continue to bake and stir until flavors are married (usually 60-90 minutes total baking time).
- ✓ Remove sauce from oven.
- ✓ Add fresh herbs (if using fresh).
- ✓ Pass mixture through a ricer and make final adjustments to seasoning. (If using a food processor, be sure to strain the sauce.)

This sauce is a delicious pasta sauce, or it can be used as the base for a meat or mushroom sauce. With the addition of fresh basil and croutons, it makes a wonderful roasted tomato soup; with the addition of half-and-half, it's transformed into a delicious cream of tomato soup. This sauce is also terrific with a hearty roasted pork chop served on a bed of faro and summer squash.

Ristorante Italiano

Noni, the mother of one of my Italian friends, comes to the West Coast once a year for a visit. Each time, she ships ahead her sauce pan, via UPS Overnight. (Insured, even.) The reason? Noni whips up gallons of sauce when she's here, and she's adamant that it just isn't right without her favorite pan.

That's how it feels at Ristorante Italiano, where they've been serving up traditional Italian dishes and pasta specialties since 1980. It's authentic. It's delicious. And it's the kind of food that's no doubt prepared in a proprietary pan.

Chicken and veal specialties, steak, local seafood, fresh (and creative) salads, and of course pasta! In addition to an extensive selection of Italian and California wines, Ristorante Italiano offers full cocktail service. Their décor is traditional Italian, and their outdoor patio has a stunning three-story mural. This is one mural that has to be seen to be believed.

Of course, one of the reasons I like visiting Ristorante Italiano is, I was born in the building, when it used to be Santa Cruz Hospital. It's where I had my first meal, after all—so dining at Ristorante Italiano is like coming home.

Voted best Italian restaurant in the county by Good Times.

The Chicken Piccata is the best I've ever had.

Ristorante Italiano
Branciforte Plaza
555 Soquel Avenue, Suite 150
Santa Cruz
458-2321

Check out the hall display listing every child born at the hospital. There're two Geezer Chicks listed...

Dinner nightly
Lunch Monday – Friday

Ristorante Italiano's

Pasta Parma

Ingredients

1 C prosciutto, sliced paper thin
4 C whipping cream
1/2 C peas
1/2 C freshly grated Parmesan cheese
1 C grated mozzarella cheese
1/4 C fresh parsley, chopped
8 C rigatoni, precooked

Preparation

- ✓ Preheat oven to 350°.
- ✓ In a medium saucepan, reduce the cream by half.
- ✓ Add the prosciutto, peas, pasta, mozzarella, Parmesan cheese, and parsley.
- ✓ Stir to mix.
- ✓ Bake in 8-oz, individual casserole dishes for 10 minutes.
- ✓ Broil until cheese is bubbly.

Serves 4

Sanderlings

Sanderlings may promote itself as "casual resort dining," but this is your destination if you're planning a special "dress up" celebration. Sanderlings offers an elegant setting with panoramic views of Monterey Bay, with consistently wonderful food and unhurried service.

It's where I've enjoyed numerous corporate Christmas lunches, dining on savory food and champagne, well into the late afternoon. Just as you might expect from a resort restaurant, the tone at Sanderlings is *relax and enjoy*. (The trick, of course, is finding your car after all that relaxation.)

Executive Chef Karl Staub offers lush food to complement the lush views: fresh seafood, local produce, and one of the finest wine lists around. And their clam chowder? Award winning and not to be missed. Sanderlings offers a veritable who's who of seafood, everything from crab cakes to sand dabs to lobster, with creative combinations of flavors. (Check out the Asian Lobster Salad on the next page.) Of course, there's filet mignon and rack of lamb for all you meat eaters, as well as vegetarian dishes.

Next time you want to dress up for a sumptuous, lingering meal, give Sanderlings a try.

Their salads and sandwiches are excellent.

I chose Sanderlings for my kids' graduation celebration, and they did a fantastic job for my family.

Sanderlings
Seascape Resort
One Seascape Resort Drive
Aptos
662-7148

Breakfast, lunch, and dinner daily
Brunch Sunday

Sanderlings'

Asian Lobster Salad

Ingredients

For the lobster

1 8 oz rock lobster tail
2 cups extra virgin olive oil
1 sprig each: Italian parsley, thyme, chive
1 shallot, chopped
1 garlic clove, crushed
1 bay leaf
3 black peppercorns
1 t salt

For the salad

1 mango, sliced thinly
1 green onion, sliced on the bias
1/4 red onion, sliced thinly
1 shallot, sliced thinly
1/3 English cucumber, sliced julienne
small bunch of micro greens
small bunch of cilantro, chopped
1 t chopped ginger
1/4 red bell pepper, sliced julienne
l orange, segmented
1 lime, segmented
6 snow peas, sliced julienne

Preparation

- ✓ Gently place all ingredients for the lobster in a nonreactive pot and place over low heat.
- ✓ Cover with foil and cook for 10-20 minutes. (The lobster should be white in color and not hard at 120°.)
- ✓ Arrange the salad ingredients (vegetables and fruits) on a plate.
- ✓ Sprinkle with ginger, salt, and pepper.
- ✓ Top with lobster tail and dressing (recipe follows.)

Serves 2

Sanderlings'

Asian Lobster Salad Dressing

Ingredients

1 T ginger
1 garlic clove
1 shallot clove
1/2 C soy sauce
1/2 C rice vinegar
1 T cilantro
1 t lime zest
1 t orange zest
1 T orange juice
salt and pepper
1 C oil (from poaching lobsters)

Preparation

- ✓ Place all ingredients except the oil in a blender.
- ✓ Blend at high speed, slowly adding the oil, until the dressing is homogenous.

Sanderlings'

Heirloom Tomato

with Cannellini Beans

Ingredients

1 large Heirloom tomato
1 C Cannellini beans
aromatics (such as onion, Italian parsley, garlic, thyme, bay leaf)
1 carrot
1 celery stalk
1 red bell pepper
1 small bunch each: Italian parsley, basil, chives
1/4 C red wine vinegar
salt and pepper

For the dressing
1/2 C walnut oil
1/4 C powdered sugar
1 shallot
1/4 C Dijon mustard
1/4 C champagne vinegar
salt and pepper to taste

Preparation

- ✓ Place beans, aromatics, and 6 cups lightly salted water in a nonreactive pan and turn heat on high.
- ✓ Cook until beans are tender (1-2 hours). Add water, if necessary.
- ✓ Place all of the dressing ingredients, except the oil, in a blender.
- ✓ Turn the blender on high and slowly add the oil. Blend until the dressing is homogenous.
- ✓ Cut the carrot, celery, and red pepper into small cubes.
- ✓ Finely mince the parsley, basil, and chives.
- ✓ Combine the beans, the cubed vegetables, and the minced herbs with the red wine vinegar.
- ✓ Salt and pepper to taste.
- ✓ Hollow out the Heirloom tomato, reserving the top for a lid.
- ✓ Salt and pepper the tomato.
- ✓ Brush the tomato with a little oil, inside and out.
- ✓ Fill the tomato with the bean mixture.
- ✓ Serve with dressing.

Serve 1

Scopazzi's

Scopazzi's has been a Santa Cruz landmark since 1915, when it was the Locatelli Hotel, a boarding house for loggers. In 1920, the redwood dining room was added, and the hotel quickly became a favorite hangout for movie stars such as Mary Pickford and Henry Fonda. 1920 also marked the start of prohibition, and according to local lore, the hotel was THE place to obtain hooch from the local stills. (Hmmm... loggers, movie stars, illegal booze – no wonder it's a landmark!)

In 1955, the Scopazzi family purchased the boarding house and converted it into the restaurant that still bears its name. Owners Talal Janbay and Paul Violante took over in 1986, continuing Scopazzi's tradition of excellent Italian food and incomparable service.

Scopazzi's serves the best Caesar salad and cannelloni in the bay area, as well as homemade desserts and traditional dishes such as veal, steak, pasta, and seafood.

The main dining room is the original, featuring tons of redwood (literally) and an A-frame ceiling. Cozy fireplaces in the main dining room and bar set the perfect tone for a winter meal.

Dining at Scopazzi's is like taking a step back in time. Only now, you can sip your glass of wine without having to keep an eye on the back exit.

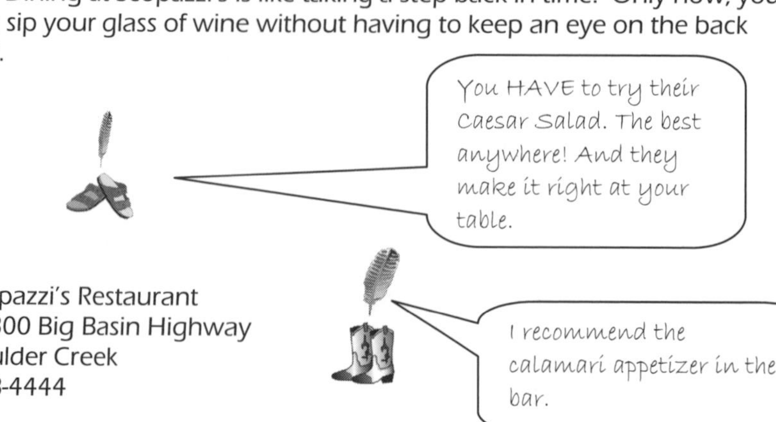

You HAVE to try their Caesar Salad. The best anywhere! And they make it right at your table.
I recommend the calamari appetizer in the bar.

Scopazzi's Restaurant
13300 Big Basin Highway
Boulder Creek
338-4444

Lunch and dinner Wed – Sun

Scopazzi's

Prosciutto Goat Cheese Wrapped Prawns

(with Red Pepper Aioli)

Ingredients

10 prawns (around 1 lb)
10 thin slices of prosciutto di parma
5 oz goat cheese
1 bunch fresh basil, chopped
2 cloves garlic, finely chopped
2 T sour cream
1/4 C olive oil
4 oz butter
salt and pepper

Preparation

- ✓ Preheat oven to 350°.
- ✓ Peel prawns and lay them flat on a work surface.
- ✓ Slice down the back of each prawn, making a small pocket. (Do not cut through the prawn.)
- ✓ Whip the goat cheese, sour cream, half of the basil, half the garlic, and a little salt and pepper into a smooth sauce.
- ✓ Transfer to a pastry bag and pipe into the back of the prawns.
- ✓ Place the prawns in a 10″ x10″ baking pan and chill for one hour.
- ✓ Lay prosciutto out on a work surface.
- ✓ Wrap one slice of prosciutto around each prawn so that it adheres.
- ✓ Place prawns back in baking pan.
- ✓ Melt butter over low heat; add olive oil, the remaining basil, and the remaining garlic.
- ✓ Pour over prawns and bake for 10-15 minutes, basting often.

Chef Paul likes to serve the prawns tail-side up around Peruvian blue mash potatoes, with snow peas between the prawns, and red pepper aioli drizzled over the dish. (Red Pepper Aioli recipe follows.)

Serves 2-3

Did you know?

Boulder Creek began as a thriving logging community in the mid 1800s, when loggers clear cut nearly every tree in sight.

Boulder Creek was hard hit by the 1989 Loma Prieta earthquake, with many residents losing their homes.

Boulder Creek averages over 54 inches of rain per year (which is why the redwoods love this area).

The inspiration for this prawns recipe came to Chef Paul Violante one day when he was sailing. (No, he wasn't sailing in Boulder Creek.)

Scopazzi's

Red Pepper Aioli

Ingredients

I large red bell pepper
1 egg
1 C soy bean oil
1 small clove garlic
a little salt and pepper

Preparation

- ✓ Roast the red pepper over gas flame or under broiler until charred.
- ✓ Place in plastic bag for 10 minutes to soften the peel.
- ✓ Peel pepper and place in blender.
- ✓ Blending at low speed, add the egg, the soy bean oil, the garlic, and the salt & pepper.
- ✓ Blend until the consistency is even.

Sestri

The Italian families who settled in Santa Cruz in the early 1900s had a deep love for entertaining friends and family. They were artists in the kitchen, creating gourmet meals with the bounty surrounding them—the fresh local produce, the gifts from both the earth and the sea. This talent and respect has been passed down through the generations of the Olivieri family, who, along with partner/chef James Smith, own and operate Sestri.

Sestri is an elegant, old-world Italian restaurant, with fine linens on the tables, lovely glassware, vibrant art on the walls. Yet, it feels like holiday dinner at Grandmother's house, with the ritual of the meal preparation and the lively conversation of family being reunited. (In fact, if you want an intimate dinner, be sure to ask for a table in the back dining room. The front room, much like Grandmother's house, can get fairly noisy when packed—which is often.)

And what about the food? You'll find familiar Italian dishes with unexpected surprises. The Piatti Del Giorno is to die for, and my favorite seafood pick is the Risotto con Frutti di Mare (seared Atlantic scallops over lemon risotto with rock shrimp, sweet peppers and basil oil). The wood-fired oven and rotisserie assure perfectly prepared meats, such as the spit-roasted pork loin or the smoked New York Steak. And the salads are especially well prepared and tasty. (By the way, the menu changes monthly to reflect the seasonal choices.)

Matching the excellent food is a terrific selection of local and Italian wines, served by the bottle or the glass. Wednesday nights are "Wine Down" night, where the patio is open for live music, great food, and (of course) wine.

Sestri is named for Santa Cruz's sister city Sestri Levante in Italy. All I can say is, "Good going, sis!"

Their New York Steak is PERFECT.

Sestri
655 Capitola Road
Santa Cruz
479-0200

Dinner nightly

Sestri's

Salmon (Gravalax)

Ingredients

1 salmon fillet (skin on, pin bones removed, cleaned, trimmed, and scored)
2 lb salmon cure (recipe follows)
salmon marinade (recipe follows)
2 lb fennel fronds

For the salmon cure
1 lb salt
3/4 lb sugar
2 oz peppercorns
1 oz star anise
1 oz cinnamon stick
1/2 oz allspice
5 bay leaves

For the salmon marinade
2-3 oz shallots, sliced
Peel from 4 lemons (no pith)
1 bunch parsley, washed and dried
1 bunch cilantro, washed and dried
1/2 bunch thyme

Preparation

- ✓ Prepare the salmon cure by lightly toasting the spices in a dry sauté pan and then mixing into the salt and sugar.
- ✓ Prepare the marinade by (1) rough chopping all the herbs, shallots, and lemon zest, and then (2) chopping everything in a food processor until minced but not pureed.
- ✓ Roll the salmon in the cure and gently rub it in.
- ✓ Pat off excess cure and then coat both sides of the fillet with marinade.
- ✓ Lay half the fennel fronds on a perforated sheet pan (or cookie cooling rack) with an underliner pan.
- ✓ Place half the excess marinade on the fronds, lay the fillet on top (skin down), and cover with the rest of the marinade and fennel fronds.
- ✓ Refrigerate one day. Then turn the fillet over and marinate one more day.
- ✓ Remove all the marinade and allow the fish to dry a bit, uncovered, for several hours or overnight in refrigerator (if the fish is large).
- ✓ Now the fish can be wrapped and sliced thin for gravalax, or it can be drizzled with lemon vodka, grappa, or Lemoncello.
- ✓ The fish is also ready at this point for cold smoking.

This salmon dish will last up to a week if it is kept wrapped and chilled in the refrigerator.

Sestri's

Polpettini della Nonna Meatballs

Ingredients

For the meatballs
1/2 lb beef chuck roll, ground
1/3 lb mild Italian sausage (loose), ground
1/3 lb pork butt or shoulder, ground
1/3 lb veal cross rib or shoulder, ground
1/4 large onion
1/2 carrot
1/2 celery stalk
1/8 t chopped garlic
1 sprig parsley, chopped
1/8 t thyme, chopped
1/8 t oregano, chopped
1 C breadcrumbs
2-4 eggs
1/4 C pecorino, grated

For the sauce
1/2 lb onion, sliced
1/2 can plum tomatoes (crushed by hand)
1/4 C oven-roasted tomatoes
1/2 C red wine
1 1/2 C chicken stock

Preparation

Preparing the meatballs

- ✓ Grind all the meats together. (They should be very cold.) Return to refrigerator.
- ✓ Rough chop the onion, carrot, and celery; then process them in food processor until medium-size dice.
- ✓ Sauté the vegetables, along with the chopped garlic, lightly in oil. Season to taste.
- ✓ Set aside to cool.

- ✓ Mix by hand: meat, bread, cooled vegetables, herbs, cheese, salt and pepper to taste.
- ✓ Add enough egg to make the mixture moist but not sticky. (The amount of egg will vary.)
- ✓ Form mixture into 3 oz balls and lay meatballs on a greased baking tray about 1/4 inch apart.
- ✓ Season with salt and pepper.
- ✓ Roast in oven until well browned.

Preparing the sauce

- ✓ In a braising pan, sauté the sliced onion in olive oil until soft.
- ✓ Add the garlic and cook for 3-4 minutes.
- ✓ Add the tomatoes and season with salt and pepper.
- ✓ Add the wine and the stock and bring to a simmer.
- ✓ Braise the meatballs in the sauce for 2 hours. (You may have to cook the meatballs in batches.)
- ✓ Meatballs and sauce may now be cooled and reserved for later use or served immediately.

To serve

- ✓ If reheating, warm 4 meatballs in sauce with some extra chicken stock and butter. Cover and place in oven.
- ✓ When hot, add a pinch of oregano.
- ✓ Cook four servings of pappardelle noodles and toss with some butter.
- ✓ Place noodles in a bowl with meatballs on top.
- ✓ Spoon sauce over the meatballs and noodles and sprinkle with Parmesan cheese.

Severino's Grill

The first time I ate at Severino's, my meal was accompanied by a daydream: Scotty had just beamed me over to a luscious resort on the Big Island, where I was enjoying a delectable meal after a long day of snorkeling. It wasn't hard to imagine. Dining outdoors amid lush gardens, complete with Koi pond and cascading waterfall—well, who wouldn't feel tropical? The nice thing about Severino's is, you can experience this same feeling dining inside, thanks to the floor-to-ceiling windows and spacious construction. Even the watercolors on the wall are reminiscent of paradise (except, of course, that you're looking at a mural of Capitola).

But let's talk about the food. Severino's award-winning menu features everything from portabella piccata to prime rib and rack of lamb. And the fresh seafood! Australian lobster anyone? (Just throw a lobbie on the barbie?) There's something here for every palate. Even kids can chomp into a killer grilled cheese sandwich. It's no wonder that Severino's motto is Get Hooked.

Locally owned and operated, Severino's also offers sunset dinners (with discounted prices) as well as one of the best happy hours around. And when you're ready to return to the mainland, just have Scottie beam you home.

You can burn off that dinner with some swing dancing on weekend nights.

This recipe was created by chef Antonio Gomez and is one of Severino's best sellers!

Severino's Grill
7500 Old Dominion Court
Aptos
688-8987

Breakfast, lunch, & dinner daily

Severino's

Antonio's Herb Stuffed Chicken

Ingredients

1 whole chicken breast
2 oz goat cheese
4-5 leaves of fresh basil, chopped
1/4 C buttermilk
1/2 C Italian-style bread crumbs
1/2 C vegetable oil
salt and pepper to taste

Preparation

- ✓ Pound chicken breast flat.
- ✓ Fill breast with goat cheese and basil.
- ✓ Roll up breast and soak in buttermilk for 10 minutes.
- ✓ Roll breast in bread crumbs.
- ✓ Sauté in vegetable oil until golden brown and cooked through.
- ✓ Remove from heat and top with mushroom cream sauce.

Serves 1

Mushroom Cream Sauce

Ingredients

1 t butter
1/2 C heavy cream
1/2 t chopped garlic
1/4 C white wine
1/2 t chopped parsley
1/2 C sliced mushrooms

Preparation

- ✓ Sauté parsley, mushrooms, and garlic in butter for 5 minutes
- ✓ Add cream and white wine; bring to a boil.
- ✓ Stir, continuing to cook until sauce thickens (about 5 minutes).
- ✓ Add salt and pepper to taste.

Shadowbrook

Shadowbrook is a Capitola institution and quite likely the most romantic restaurant in the county. For your first visit to Shadowbrook, don't expect to ooh and aah as you drive up. All you'll see is a rather impressive stone arch. The restaurant is down the hill, along the bank of the Soquel River. You get there by walking down a beautifully landscaped and serpentine path or (ready?) by taking the nostalgic cable car. Whether walking or riding, you're transported into a forest wonderland. The Capitola beach and bustling esplanade are just a few hundred feet down the river, but you'd never know it once you're under the peaceful, cool redwood canopy at Shadowbrook.

Although many miss the old, dark and cozy bar, the bright open atrium bar does offer a marvelous view of the lush green hillside. As for your dining options, Shadowbrook actually comprises several different dining rooms and outdoor terraces on various levels—some with river views, some more private, some more quiet.

Although no one can argue the romance of dining by candlelight or next to a crackling fire, the river and hillside views are best appreciated at lunch or brunch. A last word to the wise: While you shouldn't miss a walk along the serene forest path, that walk is a stroll going down and a hike coming up. Especially after a delicious four-course meal and sinful dessert. Take your time, hold hands, sneak a kiss going down to the restaurant... and then take the cable car back up to your car. Trust me on this one.

And if you really are among the lucky ones, see about a river-view table during the Capitola Begonia Festival. Shadowbrook and brightly colored, begonia-covered floats drifting down the Soquel River—an exquisite combination.

Shadowbrook
1750 Wharf Road
Capitola, CA
831-475-1511

Dinner nightly
Sunday brunch

My parents got engaged here, had their wedding dinner here, and celebrated every anniversary here.
Now **that's** a cable car named desire.

Shadowbrook's

Pacific Rim Salmon

Ingredients

8 oz salmon filet
3 oz sesame seaweed salad
1 T ginger wasabi sauce (recipe follows)
4 T ponzu sauce (recipe follows)
1/2 C julienne vegetables (jicama, cucumber, red bell pepper, carrot)
1 T miso vinaigrette (recipe follows)
pinch black sesame seeds
lemon wedge

Preparation

- ✓ Char grill the salmon filet and brush with 1 T ponzu sauce.
- ✓ Place a mound the sesame seaweed salad in the center of the plate.
- ✓ With the ginger wasabi sauce in a squeeze bottle, make an outline of flower petals around the seaweed salad.
- ✓ Fill the petals with the rest of the ponzu sauce.
- ✓ Place the grilled salmon on top of the seaweed salad.
- ✓ Toss the julienne vegetables in the miso vinaigrette and lightly sauté to heat through. (Do not overcook.)
- ✓ Place the vegetables in a pile on top of the salmon.
- ✓ Garnish with a sprinkle of black sesame seeds and a lemon wedge.

Shadowbrook's

Ginger Wasabi Sauce

Ingredients

6 oz wasabi powder
2 3/4 C mayonnaise
1 C ginger gari (Japanese pickled ginger)
water

Preparation

- ✓ Mix the wasabi powder with just enough water to make a smooth paste.
- ✓ Mix into the mayonnaise.
- ✓ Puree the ginger in a blender with a little of the juice.
- ✓ Mix into the sauce.
- ✓ Chill.

Ponzu Sauce

Ingredients

1/2 C saki
C sugar
1/4 C soy sauce
1 C orange juice
1 oz sesame seaweed salad
1/2 T lime juice
1/4 t red chili flakes

Preparation

- ✓ Combine all ingredients in pot and bring to a boil.
- ✓ Reduce slightly and thicken with a little cornstarch. (The sauce should be syrupy but not too thick.)

Shadowbrook's

Miso Vinaigrette

Ingredients

1/2 C barley miso (light miso)
1 1/4 C water
3 fl oz (6 T) honey
1 T lemon juice
1/4T sesame oil
1/4 T soy sauce
2 t fresh, grated ginger
1 fl oz water
1/5 C canola salad oil

Preparation

- ✓ Dissolve the miso in 1 1/4 C water.
- ✓ Add the honey, lemon juice, sesame oil, and soy sauce.
- ✓ Puree the fresh ginger with 1 oz of water and press through cheesecloth into the mixture.
- ✓ Blend the mixture in a blender, adding the canola oil while the motor is running.
- ✓ Chill.

Southern Exposure

Fresh. Without question, that word best describes the feel and food of Southern Exposure. Fresh crisp linens, gorgeous fresh flowers, fresh air, fresh inviting decor and, most importantly, farm- and sea-fresh ingredients. I love this special hard-to-find restaurant and was sorely tempted to keep it "my little secret." But then I realized word of chef James Wilfong's innovative work here will get out no matter what. So I admit it, Southern Exposure is a peach of a place. Owners Ann and Charlie Confer, and daughter LuAnne, have created an exquisite backdrop for James' American-Mediterranean-cum-Pan Asian creations. And so beautifully and artistically presented, you almost hate to eat them. Almost. And you will quite likely then wish you were home so you could lick the plate.

When you walk down the stairs, across the quaint little courtyard and through Southern Exposure's full bar, you know you've found one of those "our special place" places. Windows and cleverly placed mirrors fill the dining room with light and fresh air, at least until the evening chill sets in, and then the fireplace gives off that unmistakable (and very flattering!) glow. Southern Exposure is a perfect choice for that romantic evening, celebration or special night out with family and friends. Two additional rooms are available for private parties or events, or Southern Exposure can freshen your own venue via their popular catering service.

For details of upcoming special events, to reserve a private dining room or make arrangements for catering, call the restaurant or check their website.

The carmelized onion and goat cheese tart? Heavenly.

Southern Exposure Bistro
9051 Soquel Drive
Aptos, CA 95003
831-688-5566
www.southernexposurebistro.com

Dinner Wed – Sat

Southern Exposure's

Porcini Dusted Halibut

Ingredients

Porcini powder
6 oz halibut steak
salt and pepper to taste
canola/olive oil blend

Preparation

- ✓ Preheat oven to 375 °.
- ✓ Coat one side of the steak with porcini powder.
- ✓ Sear halibut over low-to-medium heat for one minute.
- ✓ Salt and pepper to taste.
- ✓ Bake for 5 minutes.

To serve

- ✓ Place some Heirloom Tomato-Leek Compote (recipe follows) on a plate, forming a circle.
- ✓ Place Truffled-Chanterelle Flan (recipe follows) on top of the compote.
- ✓ Place halibut (porcini-side up) on top of the flan.
- ✓ Garnish with daikon sprouts and enoki mushrooms.

May be served warm or cold.

Serves 1

Southern Exposure's

Truffled-Chanterelle Flan

Ingredients

4 eggs
1 C heavy cream
3 scallion stalks, chopped
1 C chanterelle mushrooms
1 t shallots, chopped
salt and pepper
shaved summer truffles or truffle oil

Preparation

- ✓ Preheat oven to 375 °.
- ✓ Sauté chanterelles and shallots in oil; season with salt and pepper; chill.
- ✓ In a medium bowl, whisk eggs, cream, scallions, truffles (or truffle oil) together until smooth.
- ✓ Add chilled chanterelles and shallots.
- ✓ Divide among greased ramekins.
- ✓ Bake in a water bath for 25-35 minutes.

May be served warm or chilled.

Southern Exposure's

Heirloom Tomato-Leek Compote

Ingredients

1-2 bunches leeks, sliced
3 heirloom tomatoes (purple Cherokees, zebras, etc.)
4 T butter
salt and pepper

Preparation

- ✓ Melt butter on low heat.
- ✓ Add leeks and simmer on very low heat until leeks are soft and transparent.
- ✓ Add tomatoes, salt, and pepper.

Star Bene

Thanks to chef/proprietor Sandro Costanza, you'll find a terrific little Italian restaurant tucked behind those enormous flowing mounds of red bougainvillea. I've yet to catch this kitchen on an off day (and believe me, I've given them plenty of chances!). Tables in the two small and tastefully decorated indoor dining rooms sport crisp linens and fresh flowers. Those of you who enjoy eating al fresco (but resent sharing your meal with winged intruders) will particularly appreciate the charming and cleverly designed patio. This is one of those places where, just when you think you've finally decided what to order off the menu, your server starts describing the day's specials and ..."ah, could you give us a few more minutes?"

If you still can't decide, trust your server's recommendations. Sandro maintains a charming, knowledgeable and professional staff; in the course of my frequent "research junkets," I found their food and wine suggestions hit the mark every time. The small parking lot can be less accommodating during peak hours, but there's always (also free) street parking available close by.

Star Bene is easy to find, just east of the yacht harbor and Twin Lakes. But should you get lost, ask anyone who looks like a Santa Cruz lifer (yes, there is most definitely a look) for directions to Buckhart's Candy Shop. That Dutch windmill next door to Star Bene today houses a bicycle shop, but, for us Geezer Chicks (and our rippling thighs), it will always be a magical little candy shop where, at Christmas, you could actually watch them make gigantic candy canes. Luckily, Star Bene continues the "sweet" tradition in this corner of our world with a decadent not-to-miss dessert menu. Bon apetit!

I'm addicted to Sandro's veal. And his stuffed portabella mushroom appetizer — to die for.

Star Bene
2-1245 E. Cliff Drive
Santa Cruz, CA 95065
831-479-4307

Dinner nightly

Star Bene's

Strozzapreti

Ingredients

500 grams (approx 1 lb) Swiss chards
400 grams (3/4 – 1 lb) bread (soft white)
150 grams (1/3 lb) butter
2 eggs
1/4 liter (approx 1 C)milk
flour
Parmesan cheese
sage
salt to taste.

Preparation

- ✓ Cut the bread into cubes and sprinkle with milk.
- ✓ Put a weight on top of the bread and refrigerate for 8 hours.
- ✓ Boil the chard shortly and drain the water immediately.
- ✓ Allow to cool.
- ✓ Mix the bread with the eggs, chard, and salt.
- ✓ Finely chop the mixture and work it until it forms a nice soft ball. (Add flour if the ball is too soft.)
- ✓ Divide the mixture into pieces and roll them into long strips (about 1/2-inch diameter).
- ✓ Cut them into little gnocchi (whatever size you want).
- ✓ Boil the dumplings one by one until they float to the top of the pot.
- ✓ Remove promptly and transfer to a hot plate.
- ✓ Top with butter, sage, and freshly grated Parmesan cheese.

Serves 6

Trout Farm Inn

Let's be perfectly clear here. This is not a farm. It is not an inn. And the trout are history. It IS a place that's dear to the hearts of Geezer Chicks and any kid living in the area circa 1950s and 60s. It wasn't an inn or a farm back then, either, but there were lots of trout in the pond on the property. Each kid got a fishing pole and a chance to catch the trout which would, in short order, become that night's dinner.

Trout Farm Inn has had its ups and downs over the intervening years. Today, thanks to young and enthusiastic new owners committed to serving up fun dining in a family-friendly atmosphere, I am happy to report Trout Farm Inn is back.

Chef/owner Michael Schwerdtfeger's menu includes creative new seafood dishes, wonderful adaptations of ever-popular comfort food, and plenty of kid favorites. Michael also has a passion for interesting wine-food pairings and has compiled an impressive list of local wines; don't hesitate to ask the knowledgeable staff for suggestions. For those who prefer their libations with a head, straight up or over ice, there's a cozy full bar overlooking the pool.

The pool? you ask. Yes, Trout Farm Inn is also a perfect cure for the summer blahs—swim, sun or snooze those dog-day blahs away at Trout Farm's beautifully refurbished pool. There's also a cute retro concession stand for those afternoon munchies; however, as no self-respecting Geezer Chick wants to face a kitchen on a hot day, we suggest you go easy on the burgers and save room for a great meal in the dining room to cap off a lazy summer day—Trout Farm Inn style!

Call or check their website for information on special events/dinners.

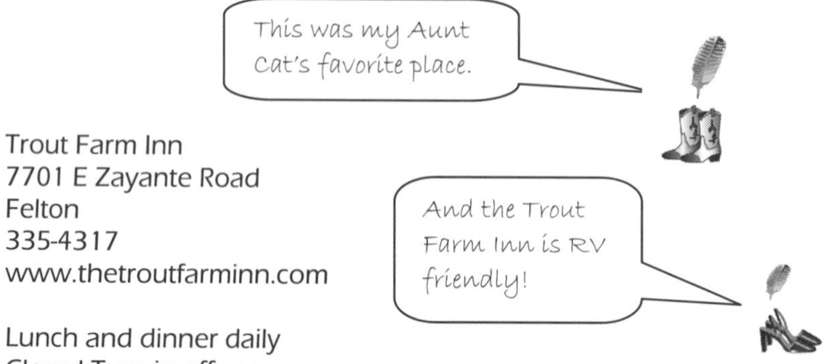

This was my Aunt Cat's favorite place.
And the Trout Farm Inn is RV friendly!

Trout Farm Inn
7701 E Zayante Road
Felton
335-4317
www.thetroutfarminn.com

Lunch and dinner daily
Closed Tues in off season

Trout Farm Inn's

Peach Scampi

Ingredients

1 lb (about 16 – 20) shrimp; peeled, cleaned, and deveined
2 C sundried peaches, sliced
1 C Maui onions, sliced
1 C peach Schnapps
1/4 lb butter, softened to room temperature
2 oz olive oil

Preparation

- ✓ In a large sauté pan, heat olive oil until smoking hot.
- ✓ Add shrimp and sauté until orange on both sides.
- ✓ Add peaches and onions; sauté until soft.
- ✓ Add peach Schnapps and flambé until flame goes out.
- ✓ Pull off heat and add butter.
- ✓ Toss until the butter is melted and the sauce is creamy.
- ✓ Serve immediately.

This dish is best served with rice and fresh vegetables... and a dry Chardonnay is perfect.

Serves 4

Tyrolean Inn

Other than actually being situated in the county, there is nothing Santa Cruz—or even California—about this little gingerbread gem. This is pure Sound of Music, oompah-oompah and cuckoo clocks magically dropped into a redwood groove where owners Whitney Parker and Chuck Cheatham offer up Bavarian cuisine (think mélange of the best of German, Austrian, French and Italian cooking). In addition to the main dining room, there's a large outdoor beer garden to enjoy on warm summer evenings under the redwoods and a sunny atrium room to enjoy year 'round. Beer afficiandos will especially appreciate the eight German beers on tap in the full bar.

With seasonal festivities throughout the year, there's always something special going on—call for details of upcoming events. Whitney and Chuck have taken extra measures to make this a truly family-friendly place with separate play areas for the kids and even an inflatable kids-only playhouse on the weekends.

If you love German food, this is your spot. If German food isn't your favorite, you're also in luck, as Tyrolean Inn's menu extends far beyond traditional German fare. And there's a dessert to satisfy every palate and sweet indulgence. For the uninitiated and grazers (those too afraid to commit to a single entree) among us, again, this is the spot. The first Thursday of every month is buffet night at Tyrolean Inn—the perfect chance to sample some of everything. The risk-eschewing among us can stay in our familiar comfort-food zone, the already-on-board can cross-gorge at will, and we all leave planning trips back for full meals of the new favorites we've discovered. One trip to Tyrolean Inn and you'll know what all that darn singing was really about!

Tyrolean Inn
9600 Highway 9
Ben Lomond, CA
831-336-5188

Dinners nightly

I'd always disliked German food. Something to do with memories of a language-class field trip gone awry. But all that's changed now. The Tyrolean Inn is WUNDERBAR!

Tyrolean Inn's

Potato Pancakes

Ingredients

2 lb Yukon gold potatoes, grated (do not peel)
2 t salt
1/2 t caraway seed (or to taste)
dash of white pepper
2 oz potato pearls or mashed potato buds
1 egg, scrambled
1/4 white onion, finely chopped
juice from half a lemon

Preparation

- ✓ Mix all ingredients by hand.
- ✓ Form 10-15 pancakes, about 1/4-inch thick.
- ✓ Grill or pan fry until brown and crisp.
- ✓ Serve plain or with applesauce.

Makes 10-15 cakes

Vasili's

How can you go wrong with a restaurant where the owner lights a flaming cheese at your table? As the flames climb toward the ceiling (and you fight the urge to dive under the table), the other patrons yell, "OPA," and you suddenly feel at home.

If you liked My Big Fat Greek Wedding, you'll love Vasili's, where it's all about experiencing (not just eating) Greek food. You recall the aunt who, perplexed by the notion of vegetarianism, proclaims, 'I'll fix you lamb!"? That's what it's like at Vasili's. Owner Julie White has continued the tradition of the original owner, Vasili himself, who infused the restaurant with his personality and his dishes with authentic ethnic flavors. In those days, meals were accompanied by spontaneous Greek dancing and plate smashing. Although things are a bit more tame these days (the plate-smashing tradition has long since disappeared), the sense of fun and ethnic pride still prevail.

I tend to think of Vasili's as one part danger (respect the flaming cheese), one part earthy lusts (gorge on the chin-dripping roasted lamb), and one part tribal unity (be one with your Greekness--for at Vasili's, *everyone* is Greek).

If you want a big fat taste of Greece (that's Greece, not grease), then Vasili's is the place. It's a tiny restaurant — and they don't take credit cards. So call for a reservation, hit the ATM, and then prepare for a meal you'll never forget.

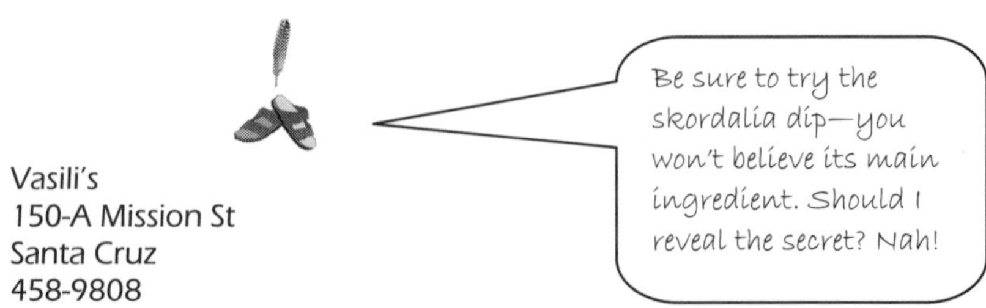

Be sure to try the skordalia dip—you won't believe its main ingredient. Should I reveal the secret? Nah!

Vasili's
150-A Mission St
Santa Cruz
458-9808

Lunch and dinner Tues– Sun
Closed Mon

Vasili's

Saganaki

(flaming cheese!)

Ingredients

2 whole eggs
2 heaping teaspoons all-purpose flour
6 oz Kasseri cheese,* in a single wedge, 1/2 inch thick
2 T clarified butter
brandy (about 2 T)

Preparation

- ✓ Mix eggs and flour together thoroughly to make a batter.
- ✓ Heat butter in pan over high heat.
- ✓ Coat cheese in batter.
- ✓ Fry cheese in the butter until golden brown and melted through.
- ✓ Remove from heat.
- ✓ Pour brandy over the cheese and then light with a match.
- ✓ Serve with bread and lemon wedges.

The flambé usually takes place at the tableside, where everyone (even pyrophobics) can enjoy the fun.

* You may purchase Kasseri cheese directly from Vasili's restaurant or through any specialty cheese shop. Kasseri cheese is also carried locally by Ben Lomond Market.

Wharf House

Strolling out to the end of the Capitola Wharf has its rewards: the lovely view, the salty scent of the ocean, and a local treasure of another kind: the Wharf House Restaurant. Locals have known for a long time that the best sheltered ocean view on a rainy winter day is the cozy atmosphere of the Wharf House. With its unblocked vistas of Capitola Village and Monterey Bay, the Wharf House is a great way to start (or end) your day. A comfy, warm décor welcomes you to spectacular views of sail boats, pelicans fishing for a meal, and seagulls gliding as they roll with the waves. It's enough to make you love inclement weather.

The house specialties are the eggs benedict dishes, and the crab Florentine is a tasty way to start your day, as well. Served alongside are homemade orange muffins and home fries. Add a glass of champagne and you have a special weekend brunch — even if the weather is boringly beautiful.

Beyond breakfast, the Boston-style clam chowder is excellent, and there's always an assortment of burgers, sandwiches, seafood treats and the old standby: fish and chips.

For dinner, the Wharf House offers outstanding seasonal specials (never overlook the Specials board!), featuring local seafood, pasta, steaks, and yummy desserts.

Whether it's the fog slowly obscuring the stars, or the dramatic drop of the sun behind the waves, or a storm kicking up some major spray, you'll find the Wharf House a perfect retreat from the elements. And as locals will tell you, it won't break the bank.

Mariedda Berbert, honorary Geezer Chick, is the world's foremost BLAT expert. And she claims the Wharf House has **the best** *bacon, lettuce, avocado, and tomato sandwich. Just remember: it's not on the menu.*

Wharf House Restaurant
1400 Wharf Road
Capitola
476-3534

Breakfast, lunch, and dinner daily

Wharf House's

Scampi-Style Garlic Prawns

Ingredients

1 T garlic, chopped
1 oz white wine
1 oz cream
1 oz butter
1/4 C mushrooms, sliced
1/4 C leeks, sliced
1 T Parmesan cheese
1 T parsley, chopped
6 medium prawns, cleaned and deveined
1 pinch Italian seasoning
salt and pepper to taste
linguini (enough for a one serving)

Preparation

- ✓ Cook linguini according to directions on package.
- ✓ Sauté prawns with garlic and butter.
- ✓ Add mushrooms, leeks, cream, Italian seasoning, salt and pepper.
- ✓ Continue cooking until leeks and mushrooms are soft.
- ✓ Serve over linguini; garnish with parmesan cheese and parsley.

Serves 1

"This recipe is certainly silly. It says to separate two eggs, but it doesn't say how far to separate them."

Gracie Allen

If there are restaurants you would like added in subsequent editions...

If you have comments about the restaurants we've included...

Or if you'd just like to contact us,

We welcome your feedback.

GCPUBS@aol.com